THE BEST OF TRADITIONAL
BRITISH COOKING

MORE THAN 70 CLASSIC STEP-BY-STEP DISHES FROM ALL AROUND
BRITAIN, BEAUTIFULLY ILLUSTRATED WITH OVER 250 PHOTOGRAPHS

CHRISTOPHER TROTTER, ANNETTE YATES &
GEORGINA CAMPBELL

This edition is published by Hermes House,
an imprint of Anness Publishing Ltd
Hermes House, 88–89 Blackfriars Road, London SE1 8HA;
tel. 020 7401 2077; fax 020 7633 9499

www.hermeshouse.com; www.annesspublishing.com

If you like the images in this book and would like to investigate
using them for publishing, promotions or advertising, please visit
our website www.practicalpictures.com for more information.

ETHICAL TRADING POLICY
Because of our ongoing ecological investment programme, you, as
our customer, can have the pleasure and reassurance of knowing
that a tree is being cultivated on your behalf to naturally replace
the materials used to make the book you are holding. For further
information about this scheme, go to www.annesspublishing.com/trees

Publisher: Joanna Lorenz
Senior Project Editor: Lucy Doncaster
Photographer: Craig Robertson
Food Stylist: Emma MacIntosh, Fergal Connolly
Prop Stylist: Helen Trent
Designer: Nigel Partridge
Proofreading Manager: Lindsay Zamponi
Production Controller: Christine Ni

© Anness Publishing Ltd 2010

Previously published as part of larger volumes, *Irish Food and
Cooking, Scottish Traditional Recipes: A Heritage of Food & Cooking,
English Traditional Recipes: A Heritage of Food & Cooking*
and *Welsh Traditional Recipes: A Heritage of Food and Cooking*

PUBLISHER'S NOTE
Although the advice and information in this book are believed to be
accurate and true at the time of going to press, neither the authors
nor the publisher can accept any legal responsibility or liability for any
errors or omissions that may be made nor for any inaccuracies nor for
any loss, harm or injury that comes from following instructions or
advice in this book.

NOTES
Bracketed terms are intended for American readers.

For all recipes, quantities are given in metric and imperial
measures and, where appropriate, in standard cups and spoons.
Follow one set of measures, but not a mixture, because they are
not interchangeable.

Standard spoon and cup measures are level. 1 tsp = 5ml,
1 tbsp = 15ml, 1 cup = 250ml/8fl oz.

Australian standard tablespoons are 20ml. Australian
readers should use 3 tsp in place of 1 tbsp for measuring
small quantities.

American pints are 16fl oz/2 cups. American readers should use
20fl oz/2.5 cups in place of 1 pint when measuring liquids.

Electric oven temperatures in this book are for conventional
ovens. When using a fan oven, the temperature will probably
need to be reduced by about 10–20°C/20–40°F. Since ovens
vary, you should check with your manufacturer's instruction book
for guidance.

The nutritional analysis given for each recipe is calculated per
portion (i.e. serving or item), unless otherwise stated. If the recipe
gives a range, such as Serves 4–6, then the nutritional analysis
will be for the smaller portion size, i.e. 6 servings. Measurements
for sodium do not include salt added to taste.

Medium (US large) eggs are used unless otherwise stated.

Front cover main image shows Scones with Jam and
Cream – for recipe, see page 90. **Back**, top left: Kinvara,
Ireland; top middle: Lake District, England; bottom middle:
Ireland; bottom right: Brecon Beacons, Wales. **Front**, top left:
Teignmouth Harbour, Devon; top middle: Stonehenge, England;
bottom middle: Presteigne, Wales; bottom right: Houses of
Parliament, London.

Contents

Introduction

This book is a taste of the food and cooking of Britain, which comprises England, Scotland, Wales and Northern Ireland. Blessed with a mild and variable climate, the country boasts a mixed landscape of fertile valleys, undulating downs and dales, rugged moors and rocky mountains. There are beautiful lakes, rushing rivers and flat, salty marshlands, as well as a long and varied coastline, much of which is dramatic and distinctive.

The British diet has been influenced not only by the landscape and the climate but also by invasion and immigration, a global empire, social development and diseases, trade and technology, politics and economics, and, of course, fashion.

Indigenous ingredients

The food of Britain has a history that stretches back more than six thousand years. Before that time this temperate, wooded country would have provided an abundance of edible mammals, birds and fish, plus vegetation, roots, fruits and nuts that were seasonally available to early hunter-gatherers. As a group of islands,

Above England, Scotland, Wales and Northern Ireland share similar cuisines, but maintain strong regional variations.

isolated off the north-west of Europe, Britain was cut off by the sea from the migration of plants and animals, and from the spread of ideas and techniques as people moved about. On the other hand, for adventurous Europeans the land over the sea promised a rich living, with its fertile soil and mineral resources, and settlers arrived in wave after wave.

Imports and influences

The people of Britain have always been keen to borrow and adapt the ideas of trading partners and incomers, and this openness to new ideas was apparent as early as the Bronze Age, as goods were imported from mainland Europe and beyond. The British traded with many other regions, and in return for raw materials, such as tin, copper, corn and wool, they were importing wine and luxury foodstuffs from southern Europe even before the arrival of the Romans. With the Roman occupation came new varieties of plants and animals, and even more exotic ingredients such as spices from Asia.

Other influences were added to the mix in later centuries: from the occupying Vikings, Saxons and Normans, and from the Arabs via trade with southern Europe. In the age of exploration, foods from the New World

Below Wales is famous for its tender, flavoursome lamb, which is used in a wide range of delectable dishes.

Above The range of vegetables on offer in Britain today is very much a result of the nation's trading past.

made their debut in European cuisine – foodstuffs such as beans and tomatoes, which are now regarded as staples of British cooking. Of these, the most important was the potato, which was to have such a profound influence on the history of Ireland in the 19th century. To begin with, it was more popular there than in England, as it proved a more reliable crop than oats and barley, and it was from Ireland that the trend for planting potatoes spread to areas like Lincolnshire and Lancashire.

More exotic ingredients and cooking styles arrived in Britain as its international power grew. Tropical luxuries such as spices, sugar, coffee, tea and chocolate became daily necessities, and the administrators of Britain's far-flung empire acquired a taste for the foods they had eaten in India and the Far East. Worcestershire sauce, for example, now regarded as a typically British condiment, is a spiced fermented fish sauce that was created in the 1830s for a family who missed the cooking of Bengal. Ironically, Worcestershire sauce made its way back to the East via European restaurants in Hong Kong and Shanghai, and is now used in Chinese cooking.

Enduring rural traditions

In every age, the new foodstuffs were most readily accepted by the wealthy and fashionable, the city dwellers and the travellers, rather than the country folk. In remote rural regions, old cooking techniques and traditional ingredients persisted far longer, particularly in the highland areas of the north and west, where the people simply would not have been able to purchase exotic innovations.

In the 18th and 19th centuries rural cottage dwellers continued to cook their daily soup of carrots, onions and cabbage in an iron pot over the kitchen fire, and bake their bannocks or potato cakes on a bakestone, while the wealthy and more cosmopolitan gentry were eating turtle soup, curries, ice cream and tropical fruits. Although some of the foreign imports have survived, for the main part it is the traditional country recipes, refined over generations, of healthy, wholesome dishes from modest ingredients, that are now a valued part of Britain's culinary heritage.

The modern age

Given the richness of Britain's food traditions and the excellence of its ingredients, it seems surprising that for much of the 20th century Britain had a reputation for food that was plain and boring, consisting mainly of overcooked meat and vegetables and stodgy puddings. This decline in British food probably stemmed from the 19th century, as Victorian morality inculcated a disdain for the sensory pleasure of eating, and the largely urban population lost touch with the quality of fresh produce. The emerging middle classes, neither very wealthy nor very poor, strove to keep up appearances with grandiose but badly cooked meals, aided by the publications of Mrs Beeton (who, among other ill-judged recommendations, suggested boiling an egg for 20 minutes).

The lowly status of cooks, who were regarded as 'below stairs' staff in the houses of the rich; the consequences of two World Wars, including food shortages and rationing; periods of economic depression; and the influx of processed foods all took their toll on the quality of British cooking.

Recovery from this adverse perception of its cuisine has taken a long time, but today Britain is once more able to take pride in its reputation for excellent food, and there is a resurgence of interest in seasonal ingredients of high quality. The nation has the ability to embrace curry, Chinese food and delicacies from around the world, while nostalgically guarding and updating its inheritance of national and regional favourites: Cullen Skink, Potted Shrimps, Cornish Pasties, Rissoles, Faggots with Onion Gravy, and the much-loved puddings that hold memories of childhood.

About this book

This beautiful volume provides an inspiring taste of the fabulous dishes that make up the British cuisine. From warming soups and delicate appetizers to satisfying main courses, flavoursome side dishes and a range of sweet treats, the traditional recipes reveal the best that Britain has to offer.

Below Britain's ancient harbours, such as Mevagissey in Cornwall, have been fishing centres for centuries.

Vegetables

Since the Romans brought their cultivated varieties to Britain in the first century BC, vegetables have played an important role in the British cuisine. In a short time the Celtic diet of wild plants and roots grew to include a range of grown and harvested vegetables. Fields of beans and peas were common by the Middle Ages, and explorers returned from the New World with potatoes and other exotics.

In most British kitchens vegetables were simply boiled and served plain, but when the landowners of the 17th century began to create kitchen gardens, cooking methods became more adventurous.

When transport improved, vegetables could be enjoyed outside their traditional growing areas, and by the late 20th century they were being imported from all over the world. Suddenly most vegetables were available all year round. Nonetheless, although modern transport allows out-of-season vegetables to be imported from many parts of the world, discerning cooks still eagerly await the arrival of the new season's home-grown potatoes and vegetables such as asparagus.

Below *In recent times there has been a growing interest in seasonal, locally produced vegetables.*

Today there is revived interest in the growing and eating of local, seasonal produce, and more shops and farmers' markets are offering high-quality local produce that hasn't been transported for hundreds of miles.

Cooking vegetables

Although vegetables and potatoes have always been important in the traditional British diet they have most often been served as side dishes to accompany meat and fish, rather than being the central feature of a main dish. They were most often boiled and usually dressed with a little butter.

Traditional soups and stews depend upon a high vegetable and herb content, but this (and a tradition of one-pot cooking) tended to encourage the cooking of vegetables for too long. This has now been remedied, however, and cooking times reduced so that vegetables retain their texture.

As well as accompanying main dishes, vegetables are used in soups, in first courses, as garnishes for entrées, as vegetarian dishes, and in many savoury dishes. In traditional British kitchens, carrot, onion, celery, leek, parsnip, swede (rutabaga), with fresh parsley, thyme, garlic and bay leaf, are collectively known as pot herbs. A mixture of these basic ingredients is at the heart of many stews and soups, and in Irish cooking it is often used as a 'bed' that absorbs juices when roasting red meats.

Beneath the soil

Carrot Every cook's standby for a side dish to accompany meat or fish, carrots are also used to give their flavour and sweetness to soups and casseroles. In the days when sugar was still a costly imported luxury, most people relied on honey to sweeten their food, but they also used the natural sweetness of root vegetables, particularly carrots. This,

together with their moist texture once cooked, makes them a successful ingredient of many delicious cakes, puddings, pies, tarts and preserves. They store well throughout the winter.

Parsnip A popular vegetable, parsnip has a distinctive, sweet flavour. Steam or boil it lightly, mash it (perhaps mixed with carrots or potatoes), roast it or add it to soups and stews. It is a perfect vehicle for spices, and makes a delicious curried soup.

Potato When the potato was introduced to Britain from America in the late 16th century, it took a long time to become accepted. However, it eventually became an important crop and by the 19th century had become a staple food throughout the nation, a status that endures to this day.

In Scotland potatoes form the basis of many traditional dishes. Mealy tatties (boiled potatoes) were cheap and filling, and were sold from carts in Scottish cites in the 19th century. Stovies is a very old dish consisting of sliced potatoes cooked with onions. Sometimes cheese or meat was added to make the dish more substantial. In Orkney cooked potatoes and turnips or kale were mashed together to make clapshot. The curiously named rumbledethumps, from the Border region, is made with potatoes and cabbage and is a Scottish version of bubble and squeak. Colcannon is an Irish dish of boiled cabbage, carrots, turnips and potatoes mashed with butter.

In Ireland, where most of the population once depended on potatoes, they are still eaten in huge quantities, boiled or steamed in their skins ('jackets') and dressed with butter. Potatoes are also mashed with milk (or cream) and butter, with added herbs or other mashed vegetables. Traditional Irish dishes such as boxty, colcannon, poundies, champ, stampy, potato cakes, breads and potato pastry are popular, and in some restaurants they can contain surprising additions.

Turnip The sweet, peppery flavour of the white turnip is best appreciated in spring and early summer, when it goes especially well with lamb and duck. Turnips were introduced into Scotland in the 18th century and the Scots recognized them immediately as a tasty vegetable – unlike the English who fed them to their cattle. Several Scottish dishes use turnips, which became the traditional accompaniment to haggis. Mashed turnips were commonly known as bashed neeps, or turnip purry (from the French purée) by the gentry. The youngest, smallest turnips have the best flavour and texture.

Swede Larger than turnip and with a leathery purple skin, swede (rutabaga) has a firm flesh and a sweet taste that is quite distinctive. It is usually eaten mashed with plenty of butter.

Onion By the Middle Ages onions, together with cabbage and beans, were one of the three main vegetables eaten by rich and poor, in all parts of the British Isles. Apart from their use in all kinds of soups and stews, they can be eaten raw in salads, fried, boiled in milk, roasted (sometimes with a cheese topping) or chargrilled. Sliced onions fried in butter until deep brown are a traditional accompaniment to steak.

Horseradish When freshly grated and mixed with cream and seasoning, this pungent root makes a sauce that is a perfect accompaniment to roast beef.

Jerusalem artichoke This knobbly root can be served roasted, boiled, or made into soup. It has an affinity with game.

Beetroot (beet) Often cooked and pickled, it can also be boiled or roasted and served hot.

Above the soil

Leek and spring onion (scallion) With its delicate onion flavour, the leek is good in many dishes, including soups, pies, sauces and stews. Leek is often used to flavour fish in the same way

Above Turnips are best served mashed or in casseroles.

that onion is used with meat. The market gardeners on the Lothian coast of Scotland supplied fruit and vegetables to Edinburgh and the quality of their leeks was unsurpassed. Scottish leeks are distinct from other leeks as they have almost as much green as white, so add a good colour to broths. They are essential to the famous cock-a-leekie soup, a broth made with chicken and leeks. Slice leeks down the middle and wash very well to remove any sand or grit. Chop and add to soups or stews.

Spring onions are used to flavour traditional potato dishes such as champ or colcannon, and in salads.

Asparagus Once known by the name of sparrowgrass, asparagus was popular with the Romans and has been grown in English country gardens since the 16th century. East Anglia and the Vale of Evesham are the traditional growing areas. It has a six-week season, which makes it a particular delicacy. It is best served steamed with melted butter or soft-boiled eggs to dip the spears into.

Cabbage One of the oldest, most common vegetables, cabbage is easy to grow. The British enjoy several varieties – green, white and red – with

Above Asparagus is available for a few short weeks in spring.

the wrinkly Savoy and young spring greens being particularly popular. Available all year round, cabbage can be boiled, steamed or stir-fried. It is the largest horticultural crop grown in Ireland after potatoes. The Irish prefer pointed-hearted, fresh, soft green-leafed types, though stewed red cabbage is a favourite accompaniment for goose and venison.

Cabbage was once a staple item of the diet in Orkney and Shetland and was eaten both on its own and as an ingredient in soups and stews. It was preserved for winter by being layered in barrels with fat, oats, salt and spices with a weight on top. It was left to ferment, the result being similar to sauerkraut.

Cauliflower and broccoli These popular vegetables can be cooked in similar ways. Favourite dishes are the classic cauliflower cheese and a soup incorporating cheese and cream. Cauliflower grows particularly well in the south-west of England.

Brussels sprouts These look like tiny cabbages but have a distinctive taste. They are served as a side vegetable (traditionally mixed with chestnuts at Christmas) or thinly sliced and served raw or stir-fried.

Above Globe artichokes look beautiful and taste wonderful.

Globe artichoke This is an edible thistle, with layers of leaves surrounding the central heart. It was introduced to Britain from the Mediterranean, but flourishes in milder regions. It is good boiled and served with lemon butter, for dipping the base of the leaves and the hearts. In spite of the name, they are not related to Jerusalem artichokes.

Celery An essential pot-herb, celery is eaten raw (as crudités), braised (especially the hearts), often with cheese, or as an ingredient in soup. After the Romans brought celery to England, it grew wild and tough until the 18th century, when it was cultivated and blanched to keep its stems tender. Now both pale green summer celery and white winter celery are enjoyed.

Spinach When spinach first arrived in Britain from Spain, where it was introduced by the Moors, it was referred to as 'the Spanish vegetable'. The small young leaves add a mildly peppery taste to salads, but it is more commonly cooked as a side dish.

Chard Though similar to spinach, chard has thick stems that can be tough when older, and need to be cooked longer than the leaves. Ruby chard has vivid red stems.

Above Crunchy, peppery radishes make a great addition to salads.

Kale Dark green leafy kale is particularly popular in Scotland, and is so central to Scottish cuisine that the word 'kail' came to mean soup and even to signify the main meal of the day. Kale grows on a long stem and has curly dark green leaves but no head. It has the advantage of flourishing in the harsher climate of northern regions and is resistant to, and indeed improved by, frost. Shred the leaves finely and cook for a few minutes in boiling salted water, as for cabbage.

Peas, broad (fava) beans, runner beans and French (green) beans
These have been grown in Britain since the Middle Ages, when they were planted in cottage gardens. In summer, peas and broad beans are deliciously sweet when small and freshly picked, or they can be dried or frozen and used throughout the winter. Beans are best simply steamed and, in the case of woodier, larger ones, shredded. They can also be added to preserves.

Pumpkin and squash Adding a dash of colour to autumn, pumpkin and squash have dense flesh, which can be roasted, mashed or used to make wonderful soups. Pumpkins are also carved for Halloween.

Salad vegetables

Cucumber Once a favourite in Victorian glasshouses, cucumbers were used to make cucumber sandwiches for refined teatime gatherings. Popular in all manner of salads and sandwiches today, they are a common sight in British kitchens.

Radish The British have eaten radishes for hundreds of years. Their peppery flavour is best appreciated when eaten just as they are, with salt for dipping.

Lettuce This first appeared in British gardens in the 16th century. Its main use is in salads, though it can be braised with peas or made into soup. There are many varieties, from traditional round and butterhead lettuces to the crisp Cos and tightly packed hearts of Little Gem.

Tomato Thought in 16th-century England to be poisonous, tomatoes are extremely popular nowadays, and are widely grown. Very versatile, they are ideal for salads, grilling (broiling), frying, roasting, soups, sauces and casseroles.

Watercress Grown in the spring waters of the south-east of England for about 200 years, watercress was commonly used to make nutritious sandwiches for the working classes. Land cress closely resembles watercress in shape and flavour and was once prevalent in the wild. It grows in winter, making it a useful standby when salad ingredients are in short supply.

Below There is a wide range of lettuces on offer in Britain.

Herbs

The Romans introduced most of the herbs the British use today. In the 16th century, when explorers brought home new exotic plants, the gardens of country houses filled with them. Some were used for culinary or medicinal purposes, or to make pomanders and scent bags.

In the Victorian era, herbs remained essential to flavour food that was often stale or bad. With the 20th century came the development of artificial flavourings, and use of herbs waned until the more recent revival of interest in seasonal and locally grown foods. Today Britain has thriving herb farms, and herbs are used in almost every savoury dish, as well as some sweet ones.

Soft herbs

Parsley This is the most versatile herb, as its leaves, stalks and roots can be used in countless ways. Its flavour goes particularly well with fish and vegetables, and it is often added to soups, sauces and stews.
Sage The strong flavour of sage goes well with cheese, potatoes and pork. It is popular as a stuffing for chicken.

Below Sage is not only attractive, but it tastes wonderful, especially in stuffings or in poultry dishes.

Above Dill works very well as an accompaniment to fish.

Mint This summer herb is chopped and mixed with sugar and vinegar to make mint sauce for roast lamb. It is also used in salads and with new potatoes.
Tarragon French tarragon is the culinary herb. Use it with eggs and chicken, and to flavour butter, vinegar and olive oil.
Dill The aniseed flavour of dill's fronds has an affinity with fish and vegetables. The seeds go well with cheese or pork.
Marjoram There are two types: sweet marjoram and wild marjoram (commonly known as oregano). Both are Mediterranean herbs, but have been assimilated into British cooking. The sweet type works especially well with roasted and slow-cooked meats, stuffings and soups, whereas wild

Below The vibrant green leaves of French tarragon add an extra flavour dimension to many egg dishes.

Above Parsley is perhaps the most widely used herb in British cooking.

marjoram has a natural affinity with tomato-based dishes and sauces.
Chives With their delicate onion flavour chives are good snipped into salads, soups, sauces and egg dishes.
Basil Frequently used in many Mediterranean dishes that are now part of the British repertoire, basil has a peppery, punchy flavour that pairs particularly well with tomatoes.
Savory Adding sprigs of savory, often called the 'bean herb', to the cooking water of any type of bean helps to prevent flatulence.

Woody herbs

Rosemary A key ingredient in any number of stews, casseroles and other slow-cooked dishes, rosemary is commonly used in British cooking.
Thyme Strongly flavoured and very fragrant, thyme is used in stuffings and, together with bay and rosemary, to make bouquet garnis. The leaves can be stripped from the woody stem or, if the whole thing is used to add flavour, the stem should be removed and discarded before the dish is served.
Bay The glossy green leaves of bay are added to a huge number of soups, stews and sauces. They should be removed at the end of the cooking time, as they are tough and will have imparted their flavour to the food.
Lavender The leaves and flowers can be used to flavour sweet dishes, such as ice creams, cakes and biscuits (cookies).

Fruits

Britain's temperate climate is ideal for growing orchard and soft fruits, and many regions still grow the varieties that they have produced for centuries.

Orchard fruits

Traditional orchards have long been a distinctive feature of the landscape, but recent years have seen a severe decline in orchard-fruit crops and many old varieties have disappeared. Fortunately, traditional fruit growers are now beginning to see a turnaround, with some supermarkets responding to consumers' demand for home-grown produce, and local shops and farmers' markets helping to bring back traditional varieties.

Apples The ancestor of the modern apple is the crab apple, with its small sour fruits that make delicious jellies and other preserves. There is a huge range of traditional apple varieties, each with its own texture and unique flavour, and many are evocatively named. Dessert apples include Ashmead's Kernel, Blenheim Orange, Cox's Orange Pippin, Discovery, James Grieve, Knobby Russet and Worcester Pearmain. Varieties that are more suitable for cooking include Bramley's Seedling, Burr Knot, Golden Hornet, Norfolk Beauty and Smart's Prince Arthur. English cider apples

Below The apple is Britain's oldest and most loved fruit.

Above Pears range from soft, juicy, sweet dessert types to firmer cooking varieties.

include Bulmer's Norman, Hoary Morning and Slack-me-girdle. Apple traditions such as apple bobbing and toffee apples survive to this day.

Pears The pear's history can be traced back almost as far as the apple's, and for a long time it was considered the superior fruit. By the 19th century there were hundreds of varieties. Today the most popular British dessert pear is the Conference, long and thin with green skin tinged with russet, and sweet flesh. Williams pears (known as Bartlett in the USA and Australia), bred in Berkshire in the 18th century, are golden yellow or red-tinged and are ideal for cooking.

Plums Originally cultivated from hedgerow fruits – the cherry plum and the sloe (black plum) – plums vary in colour from black to pale green and yellow and can be sweet or tart. In Britain they were grown in the gardens of medieval monasteries. The Victoria plum was first cultivated in Sussex in the 1800s and, with its red and yellow skin, remains the most popular dessert plum. The greengage is a sweet amber-coloured plum that makes

Above Plums are popular cooked in pies, crumbles and puddings.

particularly good jam. Damsons are small plums with dark blue-to-purple skins and yellow flesh. They give their colour and flavour to damson gin.

Cherries These are grouped into three main types: sweet, acid and sour (known as Dukes). Sweet cherries can be firm and dry, ideal for candying into glacé cherries, or soft and juicy. Acid cherries, of which the Morello is the

Below Fruit pies, in particular apple, are a favourite traditional dessert.

best known, range in colour from pale to those with an intense crimson glow. Duke cherries are thought to be a cross between these two.

Quince The quince is an apple- or pear-shaped fruit with scented yellow flesh. Because it is very hard it needs long slow cooking. It is lovely cooked with apples or pears, when only a small amount is needed to add its flavour. Quinces make good jams and jellies that go well with pork.

Berries, currants and rhubarb

Local farmers' markets and pick-your-own farms are the best sources of traditional varieties of soft fruit. All types of berry are delicate and very perishable so keep them in the refrigerator and eat them as fresh as possible. Farm shops offer good value, as the berries are usually freshly picked. Look for firm, plump berries, but remember that very large ones often lack flavour. To enjoy them at their best, allow them to reach room temperature before eating. Don't wash them until just before eating. Rinse strawberries very gently and hull them only after washing to avoid making them soggy – the hull acts as a plug.

Below Strawberries and cream are an important part of a British summer.

Above Growing wild on autumn hedgerows, blackberries are now also cultivated for sale year-round.

Strawberries These luscious berries are firmly associated with the English summer. Though Elsanta is now the most frequently grown variety, Cambridge Favourite, English Rose, Hapil and Royal Sovereign are becoming popular again. Strawberries are a traditional feature of the Wimbledon tennis championships.

Raspberries These are Scotland's national favourite, and Tayside is famous for its sweet fruits, which have been grown commercially since the beginning of the 20th century. New varieties such as Glen Moy and Glen Garry have recently been developed.

Blackberries Glossy, juicy blackberries are one of late summer's most delicious fruits, and the most common wild berry in Britain. Blackberries are also known as brambles and in the Scottish Highlands the bush is called *an druise beannaichte* – the blessed bramble.

Tayberries A cross between the red raspberry and a strain of blackberry, tayberries are very juicy with a sharp taste and make particularly good jam.

Mulberries These are similar to, though larger than, blackberries. They are the fruit of large, long-lived trees of Asian origin, which have probably been grown in England since Roman times. Mulberries are very soft and easily damaged so are not widely available.

Currants Blackcurrants, with their rich, tart flavour, are the most common currants. Red and white currants are mixed with other summer fruits in a summer pudding.

Above Redcurrants are often added to dishes or used as a pretty garnish.

Gooseberries Different varieties of these pale berries are suitable for cooking or eating raw. Gooseberries ripen when the elder tree is in flower, and elderflowers are traditionally added to impart a delicious muscatel flavour.

Rowanberries These tiny, bright orange-red berries are added to sauces and relishes for rich game meats.

Rhubarb Though botanically a vegetable, rhubarb is used like a fruit. The tender pink stems of early forced rhubarb are a spring treat, mostly grown in Yorkshire. Main crop rhubarb, with its stronger colour and more acidic flavour, is eaten in pies and crumbles.

Below Beautiful pale green gooseberries come into season in midsummer.

Fish and shellfish

Britain has always enjoyed a wonderful variety of fish from its coastal waters, lakes and rivers. Recent years have seen fish stocks diminish, but an increase in fish farming has led to greater availability of certain species such as salmon and trout. Not all the fish caught in British and Irish waters are landed there; many are eagerly bought for immediate export to Europe.

Historically, fish was eaten on the Church's many 'fast days' (including Friday every week) and during the lengthy fasts of Lent and Advent, when meat was forbidden. In Ireland this restriction affected the majority of the population until very recently, leading to an ambivalent attitude to fish, but over the past 30 years it has once again regained its place as a prized, if increasingly expensive, everyday food.

Cooking fish

Fresh fish benefits from simple methods of cooking, such as frying, grilling (broiling), steaming or baking. In restaurants fish is frequently served with classic (often French) sauces, but the vegetation from the natural habitat of the fish, and perhaps on which the fish feeds, often makes the best accompaniment.

Freshwater fish from clean waters need only simple cooking and delicate herbs, perhaps with melted butter, to bring out their natural taste. Sea fish can take more robust seasonings and ingredient pairings, and oily fish such as herring and mackerel are often cooked coated in oatmeal, which absorbs their strong flavours.

Sea fish

Several species have been affected by overfishing and stocks are desperately low. Cod and haddock are two examples of species where reduced numbers have led to higher prices. Nevertheless, both remain popular. Haddock, which is smaller than cod, has a pronounced flavour that many people consider to be finer, and in the north-east of England it is always the first choice for fish and chips. Both haddock and cod are good baked, poached, grilled or fried. Other white fish include hake, with its firm flesh, pollack, whiting and coley, all of which are excellent in pies, soups and stews.

Plaice is a popular flat fish with a good flavour and texture. Dover sole has a firm texture and a fine flavour that is best appreciated when it is simply grilled (broiled) on the bone, perhaps with melted butter, chopped parsley and lemon juice. Lemon sole has softer flesh and a flavour not quite as fine as that of Dover sole, but it too is popular, being less expensive and suitable for serving with strongly flavoured sauces.

Turbot is considered by many to be the aristocrat of fish, with a sweet flavour and firm white flesh that can stand up to robust kinds of cooking. Halibut is widely available; it is best for grilling, frying or baking, but it can be poached or steamed, too.

Herrings, sprats, pilchards, sardines and whitebait all have a similar texture and bold flavours. Britain's thriving herring industry ensured they were always cheap and they remain good value today. The larger fish

Above Salmon steaks are very versatile and can be cooked in many ways.

are delicious fried, grilled or baked. Tiny whitebait are deep-fried and eaten whole, and remain a popular appetizer in restaurants, particularly in London, where they were once so plentiful that they were sold from barrows in the streets. The pilchard has long been a mainstay of the Cornish fishing industry, though in greater demand abroad than at home: most of the fish has traditionally been salted and exported to France and Italy. Nowadays, with smaller catches and higher prices, the fresh fish is being more alluringly re-marketed in England under the name 'Cornish sardine'. Mackerel also remains inexpensive and is delicious when very fresh.

Several other species are still caught around the coast, including brill, dabs, skate, sea bass, monkfish, ling, John Dory, gurnard and red mullet.

Freshwater fish

Britain's rivers used to teem with fish, and most large country estates would have had at least one pond stocked with perch, pike and other species. Salmon is one of today's most popular fish due to the dramatic increase in fish farming around

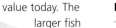

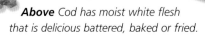

Above Cod has moist white flesh that is delicious battered, baked or fried.

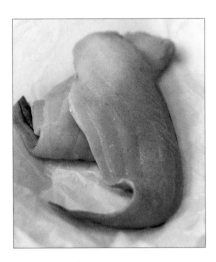

Above Smoking fish, such as haddock, preserves and flavours it.

Britain. Cooked whole it is a favourite centrepiece for summer entertaining. Fillets and steaks are lovely pan-fried, grilled or cooked on the barbecue. Wild salmon is an early summer treat worth its high price. Wild salmon, sea trout and eels are all highly prized in Ireland.

Sea trout, otherwise known as salmon trout or sewin, has firm pink flesh and a delicate flavour, combining the best qualities of salmon and trout, but in recent years it has become scarce and is currently more highly prized than salmon. It is best lightly poached whole, delicately flavoured with dill.

The brown trout is found in lakes and streams in several regions. Due to the success of fish farming, rainbow trout is now widely available and inexpensive. Both kinds of trout can be enjoyed poached, baked, fried or grilled (broiled).

Smoked fish

Before refrigeration, freezing and easy transport, smoking over peat or wood fires was one of the chief methods of preserving fish. Today fish is smoked for the flavour it imparts rather than the need to preserve it. Fish that is smoked naturally has the best taste.

Some fish, such as salmon, trout, mackerel or herring, is hot smoked, which means it is gently cooked as it is smoked and is therefore ready for eating. Cold smoking involves smoking the fish very gently over a long period over a smouldering fire. Cold-smoked fish needs either to be cooked first, as in the case of kippers or smoked haddock, or cut into wafer-thin slices and served raw, sprinkled with lemon juice, like salmon, trout or mackerel.

Though Scotland is the main British producer of smoked fish, south-west England, and Cornwall in particular, is known for its smoked mackerel, kippers and bloaters. On the east coast, Great Yarmouth once bustled with fish workers and smokehouses producing bloaters and kippers. In Northumberland smoked fish is also a speciality, especially salmon and kippers.

Shellfish

The coastlines of Britain have long been good sources of shellfish, including lobster, crab, scallops, clams and mussels. Morecambe Bay in England is famous for its tiny brown shrimps, and many sandy estuaries are home to razor clams. As with other fish, shellfish stocks have been in decline in recent years, and many sheltered bays and estuaries are now home to aquaculture farms.

Oysters were once so plentiful that they were included in many dishes to eke out the ingredients, and even as cat food, but today they are celebrated as a delicacy. Eaten raw, they are at their best from late autumn to spring – traditionally eaten only 'when there is an R in the month'. Whitstable in Kent and Lindisfarne in Northumberland are both renowned for oysters, and they are also farmed in the unpolluted waters of Scottish sea lochs on the west coast. The Pacific oyster is often used for farming and is more elongated than the native oyster.

Regarded as one of the tastiest shellfish, lobster has a rich, intense flavour. Originally eaten by the poor, it became a gourmet food in the 19th century. It is usually boiled but can also be grilled (broiled). The dark blue-green shell becomes scarlet when cooked.

Langoustines are also known as Dublin Bay prawns (jumbo shrimp), Norway lobsters or crayfish. Most fishermen regarded langoustine as a nuisance until the 1960s, when increased foreign travel began to create a demand for them. As scampi (extra-large shrimp) they became a gourmet food, exported all over the world and a fixture on restaurant menus.

Known as partans in Scotland, crabs are caught around the coasts of Britain and sold live or pre-boiled. There are two main types: the common brown crab or the rarer shore variety. The flavour of the white meat is more delicate than lobster.

Scallops have a creamy white flesh with a mild flavour, enclosed in a shell that can measure up to 15cm/6in across. The orange coral is edible and has a rich flavour and smooth texture. They need only a few minutes' cooking.

Mussels make a wonderful main dish or first course. They must have tightly closed shells; discard any that remain open when tapped (and any that stay closed once cooked). Steam or boil them in white wine or water, or add to fish stews.

Below The little brown shrimps caught in Morecambe Bay are potted and exported around the world.

Meat, game and poultry

The British have always enjoyed home-reared meat, game and poultry. For the wealthy and middle classes it was the mainstay of their diet, but the peasant class only ate it in small quantities, with maybe a joint or a whole bird on special occasions.

Before the introduction of the modern oven, particularly in large houses, meat was cooked in huge joints, roasted on a spit in front of the kitchen fire. The less wealthy would take their meat to be cooked in the baker's oven while they attended church on Sunday morning. The Sunday joint would last for several days: the leftovers would be served cold, and made into dishes such as shepherd's pie and rissoles, with the bones used for stock. While modern ovens are designed to cook smaller pieces of meat, the Sunday roast remains a traditional family and celebratory meal.

Meat

Beef Cattle are reared for both their milk and their meat. Old breeds still raised in England today include the Shorthorn (in the north) and the Red

Below The green, fertile grazing lands of Britain are ideal for raising cattle.

Poll (in eastern areas). The British White was always popular on the estates of large houses. Selective breeding means that there are now cattle suited to all kinds of terrain with breeds such as the Hereford, South Devon and Sussex providing meat that is marbled with fat and has an excellent flavour. Scottish beef from native breeds such as Highland cattle or Aberdeen Angus – both of which tolerate the bleak, rugged terrain and harsh weather – has achieved international renown for its superb flavour and succulent texture. Irish stock has also been bred from these Scottish cattle, and there the most prized beef breeds are Irish Hereford and Irish Angus; grass-fed Irish beef, like Irish lamb, has great flavour.

Beef needs hanging to develop the flavour and tenderize the meat. Good-quality beef is dark red with a marbling of creamy coloured fat – bright red, wet-looking meat indicates that it has not been hung for long enough.

These days prime cuts of beef are an expensive luxury, but roast beef with all the trimmings – Yorkshire pudding, mustard and horseradish sauce – is still a favourite. The tougher cuts, which tend to be less expensive, make delicious stews (with or without dumplings), pot roasts (such as boiled beef and carrots), and traditional puddings and pies, as well as the modern burger.

Mutton and lamb Lamb as we know it today was once unheard of. Sheep have always been raised more extensively than pigs or cattle and almost always grazed on grassland. Originally, sheep were kept primarily for their wool. All sheep meat was mutton – with a strong flavour and texture that required slow cooking to tenderize it. Over the years, lamb has replaced mutton: young, tender and sweet, it can be cooked more quickly. Lamb joints are roasted and served with mint sauce or redcurrant jelly, while chops and steaks are grilled (broiled), fried or cooked on the barbecue.

Above Beef has been associated with the British for centuries.

Today, there is spring lamb from mild southern regions, followed by hill lamb from northern areas, and lamb (up to 18 months old) from all over the country. Hogget (one to two years old) and mutton (over two years) are experiencing a welcome revival. Specialist breeds are available from farmers' markets and traditional butchers, with interesting names such as Blackface, Blue-faced Leicester, Lincoln Longwool, Norfolk Horn, Texel and White-faced Woodland.

Pork The pig has always played a most important role in British eating, and was once known in some areas as 'the gentleman who pays the rent'. There was a time when at least one pig was reared in the back yard of every cottage, farm and country house in every village and town, fed on household scraps and often on the whey left over from cheese-making. The 'porker' would be kept from springtime until autumn, when it was slaughtered. In small communities, pigs would be killed one or two at a time and the meat shared out between neighbours. This practice continued until the late 19th century.

When there was plenty of meat the people ate to 'lay on fat' before winter set in. The boar was saved for Christmas and went into minced (ground) meat pies, with the head being reserved for the table centrepiece. In the new year, the long sides (flitches) of bacon cured in autumn saw the family through the months until spring. Most parts of the pig were cured to make bacon, though the offal would be eaten immediately and some fresh pork would be cooked too. The legs were reserved for ham. Every part of the animal was eaten, including trotters (feet), stomach wall (tripe), brain, tongue, ears and tail; the blood was used for black pudding (blood sausage). Traditional breeds of pig are seeing a revival today – such as the Tamworth and Gloucester Old Spot.

Game

The eating of game once helped to sustain families through the winter months when other types of fresh meat were not available. In medieval times hunting became training for war, a rite of manhood and a traditional pastime, and was then a privilege of the wealthy and the sport of kings. While aristocrats hunted prime animals and birds, such as deer, swans, peacocks and pheasant, the peasants were allowed to hunt only small creatures.

Today, thanks to organized seasonal shoots, game is widely available from game dealers throughout the country. Scotland's wild open country has long been home to a large variety of game, of unrivalled quality and flavour.

Almost all game must be hung to develop flavour and tenderize the flesh. Birds are hung by the neck, unplucked, in a cool place. Deer are gutted and skinned before hanging. The length of hanging time depends on the type of game, where it is hung and the weather: game spoils quickly when the weather is thundery, for example.

Poultry

Chicken For hundreds of years, chickens have been bred both for their meat and their eggs, and they would have been a familiar sight in farmyards, country estates and gardens all over Britain. Older hens used to be stewed with root vegetables or made into pies, but that was in the days when they ranged freely about the farmyard, fed on a variety of foods, grew slowly and developed a complex flavour. Methods of breeding and rearing the birds have changed drastically in the modern era, and they are now plentiful and cheap.

Though most chicken meat for sale is still produced by intensive methods, there is a steady increase in the demand for free-range and organic birds, which is being met by supermarkets as well as traditional butchers and farmers' markets.

Goose Roast goose is traditional fare on Michaelmas Day (29 September), when eating it is said to bring good fortune to the diners. From September to Christmas, goose might also be served at wedding feasts and could be a regular Sunday roast for wealthy families.

Below The red deer of Scotland have long been hunted for their meat.

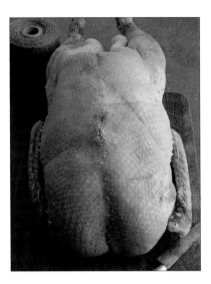

Above *Goose is a classic festive food in Britain from September to Christmas.*

In medieval Ireland, goose was stuffed with herbs and fruit, boiled with dumplings and served with apple or garlic sauce. There is no great industrial production of geese today, so the birds reared by artisan producers are a luxury food, but they are making a come-back as the bird for a special festive occasion.

Duck There are several breeds of domesticated duck, of which one of the best is the Aylesbury. Some are more fatty than others and need to be cooked for longer at a high temperature, so that the fat is rendered out and the skin crisps.

Turkey This American bird was known in Britain as early as the 17th century. Only in the 20th century, however, did it become the bird of choice for the Christmas dinner, ousting the goose as the farmyard bird most likely to generate a good income. Like chicken, modern intensive production has made it plentiful, cheap and rather bland. For the true taste of turkey, look out for birds reared by specialist producers and sold at farmers' markets and traditional butchers. The Christmas turkey is served with gravy, bread sauce, bacon rolls and small sausages, and accompanied by cranberry sauce.

Dairy produce

The dairy has always played an important part in British country life and there was a time when even small households kept a cow. In some areas a cow formed part of a labourer's wages, and they were milked on the streets of London as late as the 19th century. In addition, there would have been ewes and goats on most mixed farms. It is perhaps little wonder, then, that milk, cream, butter and a huge range of cheeses have always played a major role in the British diet, both eaten on their own and incorporated into recipes.

Milk

In some regions of Britain, such as Ireland and Jersey, cattle are raised on such fertile pastures that they produce milk with a high butterfat content. This is collected daily for pasteurization and distribution, and often undergoes a skimming process to produce full-fat (whole), semi-skimmed or skimmed milk, as well as other dairy products.

In Ireland, natural buttermilk is now mainly used for making products such as soft cheese rather than being drunk. It also remains an essential ingredient in traditional baking.

Below The British love cream, whether single, double, whipped or clotted.

In Scotland, whey and sour milk were traditionally enjoyed as refreshing summer drinks, and buttermilk was added to mashed potatoes, porridge (oatmeal), scones and bannocks. In Shetland, whey was fermented in oak casks for several months to produce blaand, a drink that has been revived and is now produced commercially.

Butter

Often found on a British table, butter is lavishly used on bread, vegetables and cakes. Produced predominantly in large-scale creameries across the region, British butter has an excellent flavour and colour. Available salted or unsalted, creamery butter is regularly sold alongside country (or farm) butter, a variation flavoured by local grasses and given a longer ripening period.

Cream and yogurt

Two types of cream are available: fresh and sour. Fresh cream – double (heavy) and single (light) – is by far the most popular, and large quantities are consumed on porridge, in coffee and poured over fruit tarts and desserts. Sour cream is used less, but is growing in popularity. Crème fraîche, originally from France, is also is now produced and widely available in supermarkets.

Left Stilton is one of the most famous and popular cheeses in Britain.

Cow's milk cheeses

Britain is home to a massive range of local and speciality cheeses. The flavour is affected by various factors, including the type of pasture on which the cows graze, the process used to create the cheese and the amount of time for which it is left to mature.

While Stilton and Cheddar are perhaps the best-known cheeses outside and within Britain, many other regional classics such as Cheshire, Wensleydale, Cornish Yarg and Red Leicester are now available from supermarkets as well as specialist cheese shops. Their texture varies from hard or crumbly to soft, semi-soft or rinded, and they have different melting qualities. Young cheeses often have a fresh, mild flavour, whereas ones that are left to mature may have a very powerful taste and aroma. Moulded cheeses have a distinctive appearance and taste, and are delicious both on the cheeseboard and in recipes.

Goat's and sheep's milk cheeses

Cheeses made with goat's or sheep's milk tend to have a strong flavour. As with cow's milk, there is a wide range of types of cheese, including hard, semi-soft and soft ones, with or without rinds. Blue and moulded varieties include Blue Rathgore, a blue goat's cheese from Northern Ireland with a slightly burnt taste, Oisin, also a goat's cheese from Ireland, and Beenleigh Blue from Devon, which is made with unpasteurized sheep's milk and is moist and crumbly.

Baked goods

Home-baking has always been important in Britain, and many people still enjoy making a range of breads, cakes and other baked goods, including bara brith (a Welsh spiced fruit bread), scones, crumpets, muffins and fruit tarts, as well as traditional sweet cakes and biscuits (cookies), such as parkin and shortbread. Traditional recipes have been handed down from generation to generation, kept alive in part by baking competitions and the Women's Institute.

Breads

In one form or another bread has been a staple of the British diet for thousands of years. In the earliest days, coarse unleavened bread was made from barley and rye as well as wheat. Later, the action of yeast was found to lighten and improve the texture of bread. Brewers' yeast was used until the 19th century, when commercially produced baking yeast became available.

Ireland is particularly notable for its bread, which is often made with bicarbonate of soda (baking soda) rather than yeast. Used with buttermilk or soured milk, the action of one enhances the other; bicarbonate of

Below Dried fruits add colour, texture and flavour to baked goods.

Above British breads include white, brown and wholemeal varieties.

soda interacts with the lactic acid of buttermilk to release carbon dioxide into the dough, making it rise. This results in the famous soda bread, which is still the bread of Ireland and is known throughout the world.

Formed into all manner of shapes, from large, rustic loaves to small, soft baps, bread still has universal appeal in Britain. White, wholemeal (whole-wheat) and whole-grain types are all popular. It is eaten on its own, as an accompaniment, sliced and toasted with various toppings or made into sandwiches. It also makes an appearance in puddings, stuffings, toppings, sauces and even ice cream.

Cakes, tarts, pies and puddings

Universally loved, there are many national and regional baked foods in Britain. Among the more well-known kinds are scones (biscuits), shortbread and parkin, and there is an endless range of pies, tarts and puddings, often made with seasonal fruit.

Butter, flour, eggs and sugar are the predominant ingredients, and these are transformed into sponges, pastries, crumbles and biscuits (cookies). Flavourings range from alcohol, used for fruit cakes and puddings, to chocolate, cocoa and spices such as cinnamon, ginger, nutmeg, cloves, vanilla and allspice.

Fresh fruits are used abundantly in tarts and cakes, as well as being preserved in the form of jams or in sugar syrup for use in dishes long after the season has finished. Crystallized fruits and dried fruits such as currants, raisins, sultanas (golden raisins), apricots, figs and prunes are often added, providing colour and flavour when the fresh types are not available. Whole, chopped or ground nuts, particularly almonds, hazelnuts and walnuts, are used in everything from breads, tarts and puddings to biscuits, cakes and meringues.

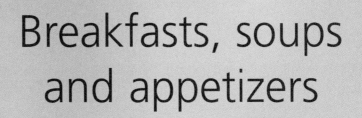

Breakfasts, soups and appetizers

Breakfast varies greatly in modern Britain. During the
week, toast and cereals are the most popular foods,
but at weekends more traditional cooked dishes,
such as poached, scrambled, boiled or coddled eggs,
kippers or a spread of bacon, eggs, sausages and
other treats, are still enjoyed. Soups, once the
mainstay of the working classes, are today more
often eaten at lunchtime or as a first course, along
with other delectable appetizers, including salads,
pâtés, mousses and shellfish.

Scrambled eggs

Carefully cooked scrambled eggs are deliciously comforting. They cook best in a pan with a heavy base. Serve them on hot buttered toast or with bacon, sausages or smoked fish.

Serves 2

4 eggs

salt and ground black pepper

25g/1oz butter

1 Break the eggs into a bowl and beat lightly with a fork until well mixed. Season with salt and pepper.

2 Put a heavy pan over a medium heat and add half the butter. When the butter begins to foam, add the eggs.

3 Using a wooden spoon, stir the eggs constantly as they cook and thicken, making sure you get right into the angle of the pan to prevent the eggs sticking there and overcooking.

4 When the eggs are quite thick and beginning to set, but still creamy, remove the pan from the heat and stir in the remaining butter. The eggs will finish cooking gently in the residual heat of the pan as you keep stirring. When they are set to your liking, serve immediately.

Poached egg

This delicate method of cooking eggs has been popular in England since the Middle Ages. Use poaching rings (if you have them) in the water for a perfect shape. Only use fresh eggs.

Serves 2

2–4 eggs

1 Put a frying pan over a medium heat and add 5cm/2in of boiling water. Add the poaching rings if you have them.

2 When tiny bubbles begin to gather in the water and gently rise to the surface, break the eggs, one at a time, into a cup and slide them carefully into the hot water. Leave the pan on the heat for 1 minute as the water simmers very gently (on no account allow it to boil). Then remove from the heat and leave the eggs to stand, uncovered, in the hot water for 10 minutes.

3 Use a slotted spoon to lift the eggs out of the water and drain briefly on kitchen paper. Serve immediately with toasted muffins.

Cook's tip Poaching pans are available with little cups for the eggs.

Energy 240kcal/995kJ; Protein 12.6g; Carbohydrate 0.1g, of which sugars 0.1g; Fat 21.4g, of which saturates 9.6g; Cholesterol 407mg; Calcium 60mg; Fibre 0g; Sodium 216mg

Energy 74kcal/306kJ; Protein 6.3g; Carbohydrate 0g, of which sugars 0g; Fat 5.6g, of which saturates 1.6g; Cholesterol 190mg; Calcium 29mg; Fibre 0g; Sodium 70mg

Boiled egg

Soft-boiled eggs are just made for dipping bread or toast 'soldiers'. In summer, they also make a delicious accompaniment to freshly cooked asparagus spears.

Serves 2

2–4 eggs

hot buttered toast, to serve

1 Put the eggs into a pan just large enough to hold them in a single layer and cover with cold water. Bring to the boil, then simmer for 3 minutes for soft-boiled, 4 minutes for a just-set yolk, or 8 minutes for hard-boiled.

2 Drain and serve immediately with hot buttered toast.

Cook's tip
To ensure the eggs do not crack during cooking, prick a tiny hole in the round end (where there is a pocket of air).

Coddled eggs

This method of soft-cooking eggs became very popular in the Victorian era, and special decorative porcelain pots with lids were produced by Royal Worcester from the 1890s.

Serves 2

butter, for greasing

2 large (US extra large) eggs

60ml/4 tbsp single (light) cream (optional)

chopped fresh chives, to garnish

1 Butter two small ramekin dishes or cups and break an egg into each. Top with a spoonful of cream, if using, and a knob of butter. Cover with foil.

2 Put a shallow pan over medium heat. Stand the dishes in the pan. Add boiling water to come halfway up the sides.

3 Heat until the water just comes to the boil then cover the pan with a lid and simmer gently for 1 minute.

4 Remove from the heat and leave to stand, still covered, for 10 minutes. Serve sprinkled with chives.

Energy 74kcal/306kJ; Protein 6.3g; Carbohydrate 0g, of which sugars 0g; Fat 5.6g, of which saturates 1.6g; Cholesterol 190mg; Calcium 29mg; Fibre 0g; Sodium 70mg

Energy 92kcal/383kJ; Protein 6.3g; Carbohydrate 0g, of which sugars 0g; Fat 7.6g, of which saturates 2.9g; Cholesterol 196mg; Calcium 29mg; Fibre 0g; Sodium 85mg

Grilled kippers with marmalade toast

Wonderful kippers are produced around the English coast, in places such as East Anglia and Craster in Northumberland, where the herrings are still cured in the traditional smokehouses that were erected in the mid-19th century. In this recipe the smokiness of the kipper is complemented by the tang of orange marmalade.

Serves 2

melted butter, for greasing

2 kippers

2 slices of bread

soft butter, for spreading

orange marmalade, for spreading

Variation Omit the marmalade and cook the kippers sprinkled with a little cayenne pepper. Serve with a knob of butter and plenty of lemon wedges for squeezing over.

1 Preheat the grill (broiler). Line the grill pan with foil – to help prevent fishy smells from lingering in the pan – and brush the foil with melted butter to stop the fish sticking.

2 Using kitchen scissors, or a knife, cut the heads and tails off the kippers.

3 Lay the fish, skin side up, on the buttered foil. Put under the hot grill and cook for 1 minute. Turn the kippers over, brush the uppermost (fleshy) side with melted butter, put back under the grill and cook for 4–5 minutes.

4 Toast the bread and spread it first with butter and then with marmalade. Serve the sizzling hot kippers immediately with the marmalade toast.

Energy 518kcal/2155kJ; Protein 33.9g; Carbohydrate 17.6g, of which sugars 5.9g; Fat 35.1g, of which saturates 7.6g; Cholesterol 121mg; Calcium 126mg; Fibre 0.4g; Sodium 1640mg

The traditional cooked breakfast

Very popular for weekend brunches and holidays, a full cooked breakfast is far more than the sum of its parts. Often comprising eggs, done in a number of ways, bacon, sausages, tomatoes and toast, it is extremely versatile and may also include mushrooms, black pudding, kidneys or potato cakes. The common factor is the tastiness and quality of the ingredients.

Serves 4

4 lamb's kidneys,
halved and trimmed

wholegrain mustard,
for spreading

8 rashers (strips) back or streaky
(fatty) bacon, preferably dry-cured

275g/10oz black pudding
(blood sausage), sliced

225g/8oz good-quality sausages

butter or vegetable oil, for grilling
or frying

4 tomatoes, halved

4–8 flat field (portabello)
mushrooms

4 potato cakes or potato bread

4 eggs

salt and ground black pepper,
to taste

chopped fresh chives or fresh
parsley sprigs, to garnish

1 Spread the kidneys with a little mustard. Grill (broil) or fry the bacon, black pudding, kidneys and sausages with butter or oil, as preferred, until crisp and nicely browned. Season to taste, and then keep warm.

2 Meanwhile, fry or grill the halved tomatoes with knobs (pats) of butter, and fry or bake the flat field mushrooms, preferably in the juices from the bacon, kidneys and sausages, until they are just tender.

3 Fry the potato cakes or potato bread until warmed through and golden brown on both sides. Cook the eggs to your liking. Arrange everything on large, warm plates, and garnish with chopped chives or parsley sprigs. Serve at once.

Energy 894kcal/3728kJ; Protein 50.6g; Carbohydrate 40.1g, of which sugars 5.5g; Fat 60.4g, of which saturates 20.1g; Cholesterol 618mg; Calcium 115mg; Fibre 3.5g; Sodium 2.25mg

Leek and bacon soup

This delicious soup is an adaptation of a traditional Welsh method of making cawl. Two generations ago, bacon, vegetables and water were put into the pot early in the morning and left to simmer over the fire all day. The bacon and vegetables were then eaten for one meal and the cawl or broth for the other. Here, everything is served at once.

3 Add the sliced leek to the pan together with the carrot, potato and oatmeal. Then bring the mixture back to the boil, and cover and simmer gently for a further 30–40 minutes until the vegetables and bacon are tender.

4 Slice the reserved dark green leeks very thinly and finely chop the parsley.

5 Lift the bacon out of the pan and either slice it and serve separately or cut it into bitesize chunks and return it to the pan.

6 Adjust the seasoning to taste, adding pepper, but please note it may not be necessary to add salt. Then bring the soup just to the boil once more. Finally, add the sliced dark green leeks along with the parsley and simmer very gently for about 5 minutes before serving the leek soup.

Serves 4–6

1 unsmoked bacon joint, such as corner or collar, weighing about 1kg/2¼lb

500g/1¼lb/4½ cups leeks, thoroughly washed

1 large carrot, peeled and finely chopped

1 large main-crop potato, peeled and sliced

15ml/1 tbsp fine or medium oatmeal

handful of fresh parsley

salt and ground black pepper

1 Trim the bacon of any excess fat, put into a large pan and pour over enough cold water to cover it. Bring to the boil, then discard the water. Add 1.5 litres/ 2¾ pints fresh cold water, bring to the boil again, then cover and simmer gently for 30 minutes.

2 Meanwhile, thickly slice the white and pale green parts of the leeks, reserving the dark green leaves.

Cook's tip
For a quicker version fry 4 finely chopped bacon rashers in butter before adding the vegetables in step 3, and use chicken or vegetable stock in place of water.

Energy 273kcal/1135kJ; Protein 18.8g; Carbohydrate 10.9g, of which sugars 3.5g; Fat 17.3g, of which saturates 6.3g; Cholesterol 53mg; Calcium 33mg; Fibre 2.7g; Sodium 1550mg

Cullen skink

The famous Cullen skink comes from the small fishing port of Cullen on the east coast of Scotland, the word 'skink' meaning an essence or soup. The fishermen smoked their smaller fish and these, with locally grown potatoes, formed their staple diet. It makes a delicious appetizer, or serve with crusty bread for a lunch or light meal.

Serves 6

1 Finnan haddock, about 350g/12oz

1 onion, chopped

bouquet garni

900ml/1½ pints/3¾ cups water

500g/1¼lb potatoes, quartered

600ml/1 pint/2½ cups milk

40g/1½oz/3 tbsp butter

salt and pepper

chopped chives, to garnish

1 Put the haddock, onion, bouquet garni and water into a large pan and bring to the boil. Skim the surface with a slotted spoon, discarding any fish skin, then cover the pan. Reduce the heat and gently poach for 10–15 minutes, until the fish flakes easily.

2 Lift the fish from the pan, using a fish slice, and remove the skin and any bones. Return the skin and bones to the pan and simmer, uncovered, for a further 30 minutes. Flake the cooked fish flesh and leave to cool.

Cook's Tip
If you can't find Finnan haddock, use a good-quality smoked haddock.

3 Strain the fish stock and return to the pan, then add the potatoes and simmer for about 25 minutes, or until tender.

4 Carefully remove the potatoes from the pan using a slotted spoon. Add the milk to the pan and bring to the boil.

5 In a separate pan, mash the potatoes with the butter. A little at a time, whisk this thoroughly into the pan until the soup is thick and creamy.

6 Add the flaked fish to the pan and adjust the seasoning. Sprinkle with chives and serve immediately with fresh crusty bread.

Energy 205kcal/864kJ; Protein 16.1g; Carbohydrate 19g, of which sugars 6.4g; Fat 7.8g, of which saturates 4.7g; Cholesterol 41mg; Calcium 137mg; Fibre 1g; Sodium 132mg

Bacon broth

A hearty meal in a soup bowl. The bacon hock contributes flavour and some meat to this dish, but it may be salty so remember to taste and add extra salt only if required.

Serves 6–8

1 bacon hock, about 900g/2lb

75g/3oz/⅓ cup pearl barley

75g/3oz/⅓ cup lentils

2 leeks, sliced, or onions, diced

4 carrots, diced

200g/7oz swede (rutabaga), diced

3 potatoes, diced

small bunch of herbs (thyme, parsley, bay leaf)

1 small cabbage, trimmed, quartered or sliced

salt and ground black pepper

chopped fresh parsley, to garnish

brown bread, to serve

1 Soak the bacon in cold water overnight. Next morning, drain it and put it into a large pan with enough fresh cold water to cover it. Bring to the boil, skim off any scum that rises to the surface, and then add the barley and lentils. Bring back to the boil and simmer for about 15 minutes.

2 Add the vegetables to the pan with some black pepper and the herbs. Bring back to the boil, reduce the heat and simmer gently for 1½ hours, or until the meat is tender.

3 Lift the bacon hock from the pan with a slotted spoon. Remove the skin, then take the meat off the bones and break it into bitesize pieces. Return to the pan with the cabbage. Discard the herbs and cook for a little longer until the cabbage is cooked to your liking.

4 Adjust the seasoning and ladle into large serving bowls, garnish with parsley and serve with freshly baked brown bread.

Energy 306kcal/1284kJ; Protein 17.7g; Carbohydrate 33.5g, of which sugars 8.3g; Fat 12.1g, of which saturates 4.3g; Cholesterol 35mg; Calcium 74mg; Fibre 4.6g; Sodium 1050g

Beef and barley soup

This traditional Irish farmhouse soup makes a wonderfully restorative dish on a cold day. The flavours develop particularly well if it is made in advance and reheated until piping hot to serve.

Serves 6–8

450–675g/1–1½lb rib steak, or other stewing beef on the bone

2 large onions

50g/2oz/¼ cup pearl barley

50g/2oz/¼ cup green split peas

3 large carrots, chopped

2 white turnips, chopped

3 celery stalks, chopped

1 large or 2 medium leeks, thinly sliced

salt and ground black pepper

chopped fresh parsley, to serve

1 Bone the meat, put the bones and half an onion, roughly sliced, into a large pan. Cover with cold water, season and bring to the boil. Skim if necessary, then leave to simmer until required.

2 Meanwhile, trim any fat or gristle from the meat and cut into small pieces. Chop the remaining onions finely. Drain the stock from the bones, make it up with water to 2 litres/3½ pints/9 cups, and return to the rinsed pan with the meat, onions, barley and split peas.

3 Season, bring to the boil, and skim if necessary. Reduce the heat, cover and simmer for about 30 minutes.

4 Add the rest of the vegetables and simmer for 1 hour, or until the meat is tender. Check the seasoning. Serve in large warmed bowls, generously sprinkled with parsley.

Above *A traditional Irish thatched roof cottage in Mooncoin village, Kilkenny.*

Energy 194kcal/816kJ; Protein 20.3g; Carbohydrate 21.6g, of which sugars 12g; Fat 3.5g, of which saturates 1.2g; Cholesterol 50mg; Calcium 84mg; Fibre 5g; Sodium 88mg

Goat's cheese salad with hazelnut dressing

Goats have long been kept in the harsher regions of Britain, where the land is too steep and rocky for cattle to thrive. The milder types of goat's cheese, such as Corleggy Quivvy and Boilié from Ireland, are ideal for using in flavoursome salads such as this one.

Serves 4

175g/6oz mixed salad leaves, such as lamb's lettuce, rocket (arugula), radicchio, frisée or cress

a few fresh large-leafed herbs, such as chervil and flat leaf parsley

15ml/1 tbsp toasted hazelnuts, roughly chopped

15–20 goat's cheese balls or cubes

For the dressing

30ml/2 tbsp hazelnut oil, olive oil or sunflower oil

5–10ml/1–2 tsp sherry vinegar or good wine vinegar, to taste

salt and ground black pepper

1 Tear up any large salad leaves. Put all the leaves into a large salad bowl with the fresh herbs and most of the toasted, chopped nuts (reserve a few for the garnish).

2 To make the dressing, whisk the hazelnut, olive or sunflower oil and vinegar together, and then season to taste with salt and pepper.

3 Just before serving, toss the salad in the dressing and divide it among four serving plates. Arrange the drained goat's cheese balls or cubes over the leaves, sprinkle over the remaining chopped nuts and serve.

Cook's tip A grilled (broiled) slice from a goat's cheese log can replace the cheese balls or cubes if you prefer.

Energy 225kcal/931kJ; Protein 11g; Carbohydrate 1.4g, of which sugars 1.3g; Fat 19.5g, of which saturates 8.7g; Cholesterol 41mg; Calcium 138mg; Fibre 1.2g; Sodium 325mg

Salad of Carmarthen ham with smoked salmon

This famous dry-cured Carmarthen ham is Wales's answer to Italian prosciutto, French Bayonne and Spanish Serrano or Iberico hams. Its flavour is rich and deep and a little can go a long way. In this salad, it is paired with hot-smoked salmon, served in a warm dressing.

Serves 4

90ml/6 tbsp olive oil

100g/3¾oz Carmarthen ham slices, cut into wide strips

4 spring onions (scallions), thinly sliced

300g/11oz hot-smoked salmon, skin removed and roughly flaked

30ml/2 tbsp lemon juice

mixed salad leaves, such as spinach, watercress, frisée, little gem and lollo rosso

1 Heat the oil in a frying pan. Toss in the ham and cook quickly until crisp and tinged with golden brown. Lift the ham out on to a plate using tongs and keep warm.

2 Add the spring onions and salmon to the hot pan and sprinkle in the lemon juice. Once warm, return the ham to the pan. Arrange the salad leaves on plates and spoon the ham and salmon over.

Energy 288kcal/1196kJ; Protein 24.1g; Carbohydrate 1g, of which sugars 1g; Fat 20.9g, of which saturates 3.3g; Cholesterol 41mg; Calcium 27mg; Fibre 0.4g; Sodium 1712mg

Mallard pâté

Mallard ducks are shot during the game season, which in Scotland is during the winter months. This recipe needs two days to prepare, as the birds need to be briefly cooked and allowed to rest overnight before making the rest of the pâté.

Serves 4

2 young mallards

a little groundnut (peanut) oil

185g/6½oz streaky (fatty) bacon

300g/11oz wild duck livers

10ml/2 tsp salt

ground black pepper

pinch each of grated nutmeg, ground ginger and ground cloves

275ml/9fl oz/generous 1 cup double (heavy) cream

4 egg yolks

37.5ml/2½ tbsp brandy

50g/2oz/scant ⅓ cup sultanas (golden raisins)

1 Preheat the oven to 240°C/475°F/ Gas 9. Remove the legs from the ducks. Season the birds and sprinkle with oil. Roast in the preheated oven for 15 minutes then remove from the oven and leave to rest, overnight if possible.

2 The next day, preheat the oven to 190°C/375°F/Gas 5. Put the bacon, livers, salt, pepper and spices into a blender and purée to a smooth cream.

3 Add the cream, egg yolks and brandy, and purée for a further 30 seconds. Push the mixture through a sieve into a mixing bowl and add the sultanas.

4 Remove the breasts from the ducks and skin them. Dice the meat finely then mix into the liver mixture.

5 Put the mixture in a terrine, cover with foil and cook in the oven in a roasting pan of hot water for 40–50 minutes. The centre should be slightly wobbly. Cool then chill for at least 4 hours. Serve with toast.

Energy 771kcal/3203kJ; Protein 48.5g; Carbohydrate 9.8g, of which sugars 9.8g; Fat 59.3g, of which saturates 28.4g; Cholesterol 636mg; Calcium 81mg; Fibre 0.3g; Sodium 1782mg

Salmon mousse

This type of light and delicate mousse often features in the wedding feasts of English brides. It is ideal for a summer lunch or buffet, garnished with thinly sliced cucumber, cherry tomatoes and lemon wedges. Serve it with something crisp – thin crackers or toast.

Serves 6–8

300ml/½ pint/1¼ cups milk

1 small onion, thinly sliced

1 small carrot, thinly sllced

2 bay leaves

2 sprigs of parsley or dill

4 whole peppercorns

15ml/1 tbsp powdered gelatine

350g/12oz salmon fillet

75ml/5 tbsp dry white vermouth or white wine

25g/1oz/2 tbsp butter

25g/1oz/4 tbsp flour

75ml/5 tbsp mayonnaise

salt and ground black pepper

150ml/¼ pint/⅔ cup whipping cream

1 Put the milk in a pan with half the onion, carrot, herbs and peppercorns. Bring to the boil, remove from the heat, cover and leave to stand for 30 minutes. Meanwhile, sprinkle the gelatine over 45ml/3 tbsp cold water and leave to soak.

2 Put the salmon in a shallow pan with the remaining half onion, carrot, herbs and peppercorns.

3 Add the vermouth and 60ml/4 tbsp water to the pan. Simmer, covered, for 10 minutes. Remove the fish with a slotted spoon. Leave to cool slightly, then flake the fish, discarding the skin and bones.

4 Boil the juices in the pan to reduce by half, strain and reserve.

5 Strain the infused milk into a clean pan and add the butter and flour.

6 Whisking, cook until the sauce thickens, then simmer gently for 1 minute. Pour into a food processor or blender. Add the gelatine and blend. Add the salmon and the cooking juices and blend.

7 Transfer to a bowl, stir in the mayonnaise and seasoning. Whip the cream and fold in gently. Pour into an oiled mould, cover and refrigerate for about 2 hours or until set. Turn the mousse out onto a flat plate to serve.

Energy 285kcal/1183kJ; Protein 12.6g; Carbohydrate 5.8g, of which sugars 3.2g; Fat 22.7g, of which saturates 8.7g; Cholesterol 57mg; Calcium 73mg; Fibre 0.2g; Sodium 103mg

Garlic-stuffed mussels

At one time mussels, along with other shellfish, were regarded as food for the poor, as they were so plentiful around the British coast. Now they are appreciated as a delicacy, and they make a wonderful appetizer with garlic and crunchy breadcrumbs.

Serves 4–6

2kg/4½lb fresh mussels

175g/6oz/¾ cup butter

4–6 garlic cloves, crushed

50g/2oz/1 cup fresh white breadcrumbs

15ml/1 tbsp finely chopped fresh parsley

juice of 1 lemon

brown bread, to serve

1 Wash the mussels in cold water. Remove the beards and discard any with broken shells, or those that don't close when tapped.

2 Put the mussels into a shallow, heavy pan, without adding any liquid. Cover tightly and cook over a high heat for a few minutes, until all the mussels have opened. Discard any mussels that fail to open.

3 Remove the top shell from each mussel and arrange the bottom shells with the mussels in a shallow flameproof dish.

4 Melt the butter in a small pan, add the crushed garlic, breadcrumbs, parsley and lemon juice. Mix well and sprinkle this mixture over the mussels.

5 Cook under a hot grill (broiler) until golden brown. Serve very hot, with freshly baked brown bread.

Above Cockles, mussels and other shellfish are a popular catch in Britain.

Energy 500kcal/2082kJ; Protein 27.7g; Carbohydrate 10g, of which sugars 0.6g; Fat 39.2g, of which saturates 23.3g; Cholesterol 153mg; Calcium 319mg; Fibre 0.3g; Sodium 675mg

Potted shrimps

Tiny brown shrimps found in the seas around England (most famously those from Morecambe Bay) have been potted in spiced butter since about 1800. If your fishmonger doesn't have them you can use small cooked prawns instead.

Serves 4

225g/8oz cooked, shelled shrimps

225g/8oz/1 cup butter

pinch of ground mace

salt

cayenne pepper

dill sprigs, to garnish

lemon wedges and thin slices of brown bread and butter, to serve

1 Chop a quarter of the shrimps. Melt 115g/4oz/½ cup of the butter slowly.

2 Skim off any foam that rises to the surface of the butter. Stir in all the shrimps, the mace, salt and cayenne and heat gently without boiling. Pour the mixture into four individual dishes and leave to cool.

3 Melt the remaining butter in a small pan, then spoon the clear butter over the shrimps, leaving the sediment behind. When the butter is almost set, place a dill sprig in the centre of each dish. Cover and chill.

4 Remove from the refrigerator 30 minutes before serving with lemon wedges and buttered brown bread.

Prawn cocktail

This 1960s dinner-party appetizer is a delight, so long as it includes really crisp lettuce and is assembled at the last minute. The traditional accompaniment is brown bread and butter.

Serves 6

60ml/4 tbsp double (heavy) cream, lightly whipped

60ml/4 tbsp mayonnaise

60ml/4 tbsp tomato ketchup

5–10ml/1–2 tsp Worcestershire sauce

juice of 1 lemon

450g/1lb cooked peeled prawns (shrimp)

salt and ground black pepper

½ crisp lettuce, finely shredded

paprika

thinly sliced brown bread, butter and lemon wedges, to serve

1 Mix the cream, mayonnaise, ketchup, Worcestershire sauce and lemon juice in a bowl. Stir in the prawns and season.

2 Part-fill six glasses with lettuce. Spoon the prawns over and sprinkle with paprika. Serve with bread and lemon.

Energy 460kcal/1895kJ; Protein 9.6g; Carbohydrate 0.4g, of which sugars 0.4g; Fat 46.7g, of which saturates 29.4g; Cholesterol 193mg; Calcium 83mg; Fibre 0g; Sodium 555mg

Energy 193kcal/802kJ; Protein 13.9g; Carbohydrate 4g, of which sugars 3.9g; Fat 13.6g, of which saturates 4.6g; Cholesterol 167mg; Calcium 79mg; Fibre 0.4g; Sodium 374mg

Fish and shellfish

Britain enjoys a wonderful variety of salt- and fresh-water fish and shellfish from its extensive coastline and its lakes, reservoirs and fast-flowing rivers. These are then baked, poached, fried, stuffed, braised and steamed with carefully chosen ingredients to produce an array of delectable dishes. From everyday classics such as Gratin of Cod with Wholegrain Mustard, or Herrings with Mustard, to more luxurious combinations such as King Scallops with Bacon, or Baked Salmon with Herb and Lemon Mayonnaise, there is something to whet everybody's appetite.

Gratin of cod with wholegrain mustard

Made with cheese and cream and flavoured with mustard to add piquancy, this easy-to-make gratin is extremely rich and satisfying and is perfect for family meals. Although this recipe uses good-quality farmed cod, you could use any thick, flaky-textured, moist white-fleshed fish, such as haddock, hake, coley or pollard, depending on what is available.

Serves 4

4 cod steaks, approximately 175g/6oz each

200g/7oz/1¾ cups grated mature (sharp) Cheddar cheese

15ml/1 tbsp wholegrain mustard

75ml/5 tbsp double (heavy) cream

salt and ground black pepper

1 Preheat the oven to 200°C/400°F/ Gas 6. Check the fish for bones. Butter the base and sides of an ovenproof dish then place the fish fillets skin side down in the dish and season.

2 In a small bowl, mix the grated cheese and mustard together with enough cream to form a spreadable but thick paste. Make sure that the cheese and mustard are thoroughly blended to ensure an even taste. Season lightly with salt and ground black pepper.

3 Spread the cheese mixture thickly and evenly over each fish fillet, using it all up. Bake in the preheated oven for 20 minutes. The top will be browned and bubbling and the fish underneath flaky and tender. Serve immediately on warmed plates.

Energy 445kcal/1852kJ; Protein 46g; Carbohydrate 0.4g, of which sugars 0.4g; Fat 27.7g, of which saturates 17.3g; Cholesterol 157mg; Calcium 395mg; Fibre 0g; Sodium 474mg

Plaice fillets with sorrel and lemon butter

Sorrel is a wild herb that is now grown commercially. It is very good in salads and, roughly chopped, makes an ideal partner for this slightly sweet-fleshed fish. Plaice – such a pretty variety with its orange spots and fern-like frills – has a delicate taste that works well with this sauce. Cook it simply like this to get the full natural flavours of the ingredients.

Serves 4

200g/7oz/scant 1 cup butter

500g/1¼lb plaice fillets, skinned and patted dry

30ml/2 tbsp chopped fresh sorrel

90ml/6 tbsp dry white wine

a little lemon juice

1 Heat half the butter in a large frying pan and, just as it is melted, place the fillets skin side down. Cook briefly, just to firm up, reduce the heat and turn the fish over. The fish will be cooked in less than 5 minutes. Try not to let the butter brown or allow the fish to colour.

2 Remove the fish fillets from the pan and keep warm between two plates. Cut the remaining butter into chunks. Add the chopped sorrel to the pan and stir.

Variation
Instead of using sorrel, you could try this recipe with tarragon or thyme.

3 Add the wine then, as it bubbles, add the butter, swirling it in piece by piece and not allowing the sauce to boil. Stir in a little lemon juice. Serve the fish with the sorrel and lemon butter spooned over, with some crunchy green beans and perhaps some new potatoes, if you like.

Energy 494kcal/2047kJ; Protein 25.7g; Carbohydrate 0.5g, of which sugars 0.5g; Fat 43.3g, of which saturates 26.4g; Cholesterol 170mg; Calcium 98mg; Fibre 0.3g; Sodium 501mg

Trout with bacon

Wrapping trout in bacon, as is done in this recipe, helps to retain moisture and adds flavour, particularly to farmed fish. If you are lucky enough to obtain wild trout you will appreciate just how well its earthy flavour works with the bacon and leek. Make sure you use dry-cure bacon for this traditional Welsh fish classic.

Serves 4

4 trout, each weighing about 225g/8oz, cleaned

salt and ground black pepper

handful of parsley sprigs

4 lemon slices, plus lemon wedges to serve

8 large leek leaves

8 streaky (fatty) bacon rashers (strips), rinds removed

Cook's tips

• This dish is nicer and easier to eat if the backbone is removed from the fish first – ask your fishmonger to do this. Leave the head and tail on or cut them off, as you prefer.

• Use tender leaves (layers) of leek, rather than the tough outer ones. Alternatively, if you want to use the outer leaves, soften them by pouring boiling water over them and leaving them to stand for a few minutes before draining.

1 Preheat the oven to 180°C/350°F/Gas 4. Rinse the trout, inside and out, under cold running water, then pat dry with kitchen paper. Season the cavities with salt and ground black pepper and put a few parsley sprigs and a slice of lemon into each.

2 Wrap two leek leaves, then two bacon rashers, spiral fashion around each fish. It may be helpful to secure the ends with wooden cocktail sticks (toothpicks).

3 Lay the fish in a shallow ovenproof dish, in a single layer and side by side, head next to tail.

4 Bake for about 20 minutes, until the bacon is brown and the leeks are tender. The trout should be cooked through; check by inserting a sharp knife into the thickest part.

5 Sprinkle the remaining parsley over the trout and serve.

Energy 324kcal/1357kJ; Protein 44.4g; Carbohydrate 0.4g, of which sugars 0.3g; Fat 16.1g, of which saturates 5.1g; Cholesterol 174mg; Calcium 60mg; Fibre 0.3g; Sodium 997mg

Baked salmon with herb and lemon mayonnaise

Years ago it was usual to poach a whole salmon in milk. Today few modern hobs have space for a fish kettle and the salmon is more likely to be cooked in the oven. Leave the head on or take it off, as you prefer. Popular all over Britain, this can be made with either salmon or trout and served hot or cold – perfect for a light summer lunch.

Serves 6

1.3kg/3lb fresh whole salmon or sewin (sea trout), cleaned

salt and ground black pepper

1 small lemon, thinly sliced

handful of parsley sprigs

butter or oil for greasing

For the herb and lemon mayonnaise

300ml/½ pint/1¼ cups mayonnaise

30ml/2 tbsp natural (plain) yogurt or single (light) cream

finely grated rind of ½ lemon

30ml/2 tbsp finely chopped fresh chives

15ml/1 tbsp finely chopped fresh parsley

squeeze of lemon juice (optional)

1 Start by preheating the oven to 180°C/350°F/Gas 4. Rinse the cleaned salmon or sewin, both inside and out, under cold running water, and then pat it dry with kitchen paper. Season the cavity with a little salt and pepper and then spread half the lemon slices and the parsley sprigs inside the fish.

2 Grease a large sheet of thick foil and lay the fish on it. Put the remaining lemon slices and parsley on top. Fold the foil over to make a loose, but secure, parcel. Put into the hot oven for 40 minutes.

3 Stir together the mayonnaise ingredients, adding lemon juice to taste.

4 Lift the fish from the oven and tear open the foil. Peel away the skin, cutting around the head and tail with a sharp knife and discarding the parsley and lemon from the top of the fish. Carefully turn the fish over and repeat with the other side.

5 Lift on to a warmed serving plate and serve the salmon with the herb and lemon mayonnaise.

Cook's tip
To serve the dish cold, leave the fish to cool completely in the foil parcel before removing its skin. This will help the salmon to retain maximum moisture as it cools.

Energy 551kcal/2289kJ; Protein 35.9g; Carbohydrate 1.5g, of which sugars 1.2g; Fat 44.7g, of which saturates 7.3g; Cholesterol 182mg; Calcium 84mg; Fibre 0.4g; Sodium 362mg

Mackerel with rhubarb sauce

Mackerel are available in Britain for most of the year, but they are really at their best in early summer, just when rhubarb is growing strongly – a happy coincidence, as the tartness of rhubarb offsets the richness of the oily fish to perfection.

Serves 4

4 whole mackerel, cleaned

25g/1oz/2 tbsp butter

1 onion, finely chopped

90ml/6 tbsp fresh white breadcrumbs

15ml/1 tbsp chopped fresh parsley

finely grated rind of 1 lemon

salt and ground black pepper

freshly grated nutmeg

1 egg, lightly beaten

melted butter or olive oil, for brushing

For the sauce

225g/8oz rhubarb (trimmed weight), cut into 1cm/½in lengths

25–50g/1–2oz/2–4 tbsp caster (superfine) sugar

25g/1oz/2 tbsp butter

15ml/1 tbsp chopped fresh tarragon (optional)

1 Ask the fishmonger to bone the mackerel, or do it yourself: open out the body of the cleaned fish, turn flesh side down on a board and run your thumb firmly down the backbone – when you turn the fish over, the bones should lift out in one complete section.

2 Melt the butter in a pan and cook the onion gently for 5–10 minutes, until softened but not browned. Add the breadcrumbs, parsley, lemon rind, salt, pepper and grated nutmeg. Mix well, and then add the beaten egg to bind.

3 Divide the mixture among the four fish, wrap the fish over and secure with cocktail sticks (toothpicks). Brush with melted butter or olive oil. Preheat the grill (broiler) and cook under a medium heat for about 8 minutes on each side.

4 Meanwhile, make the sauce: put the rhubarb into a pan with 75ml/2½fl oz/ ⅓ cup water, 25g/1oz/2 tbsp of the sugar and the butter. Cook over a gentle heat until the rhubarb is tender. Taste for sweetness and add extra sugar if necessary, bearing in mind that the sauce needs to be quite sharp.

5 Serve the stuffed mackerel with the hot sauce garnished with the tarragon.

Energy 728kcal/3034kJ; Protein 48.2g; Carbohydrate 27.5g, of which sugars 9.8g; Fat 48g, of which saturates 14.3g; Cholesterol 193mg; Calcium 129mg; Fibre 1.8g; Sodium 398mg

Herrings with mustard

The west coast of Wales was famous for its herring catches. Whole fish would be fried or grilled for serving with baked potatoes, while fillets were spread with mustard, rolled and cooked with potato, onion and apple. The latter was the inspiration for this dish.

Serves 2

4–6 herrings, filleted

20–30ml/4–6 tsp wholegrain mustard

4–6 small young sage leaves

1 eating apple

wholemeal (wholewheat) bread
to serve

1 Preheat the oven to 180°C/350°F/ Gas 4. Rinse the herrings and dry inside and out with kitchen paper.

2 Open the fish and lay them, skin side down, on a board or the surface. Spread with 5ml/1 tsp mustard and tear 1 sage leaf over each one.

3 Quarter and core the apple and cut into thin wedges. Lay the wedges lengthways along one side of each fish, overlapping them as you go. Fold the other half of the fish over the apple.

4 Oil a baking tray (or line it with baking parchment) and carefully lift the filled herrings on to it.

5 Cook the herrings in the hot oven for about 20 minutes, until they are cooked and just beginning to brown on the edges. Serve with wholemeal bread.

Energy 209kcal/870kJ; Protein 18.5g; Carbohydrate 3.5g, of which sugars 3.5g; Fat 13.5g, of which saturates 3.3g; Cholesterol 50mg; Calcium 102mg; Fibre 1.6g; Sodium 128mg

Fisherman's casserole

This is the ultimate in versatile recipes, as you can use any good-quality, fresh fish and shellfish you like. The addition of potatoes and vegetables not only adds flavour and colour but also substance, making this a substantial meal-in-a-bowl.

Serves 4

500g/1¼lb mixed fish fillets, such as haddock, bass, red mullet, salmon

500g/1¼lb mixed shellfish, such as squid strips, mussels, cockles and prawns (shrimp)

15ml/1 tbsp vegetable oil

25g/1oz/2 tbsp butter

1 medium onion, finely chopped

1 carrot, finely chopped

3 celery sticks, finely chopped

30ml/2 tbsp plain (all-purpose) flour

600ml/1 pint/2½ cups fish stock

300ml/½pt/1¼ cups dry (hard) cider

350g/12oz small new potatoes, halved

150m/¼ pint/⅔ cup double (heavy) cream

salt and ground black pepper

small handful of chopped mixed herbs such as parsley, chives and dill

1 Wash the fish fillets and dry on kitchen paper. With a sharp knife, remove the skin, feel carefully for any bones and extract them. Cut the fish into large, even chunks.

2 Prepare the shellfish, shelling the prawns if necessary. Scrub the mussels and cockles, discarding any with broken shells or that do not close when given a sharp tap. Pull off the black tufts (beards) attached to the mussels.

3 Heat the oil and butter in a large pan, add the onion, carrot and celery and cook over a medium heat, stirring occasionally, until beginning to soften and turn golden brown. Add the flour, and cook for 1 minute.

4 Remove the pan from the heat and gradually stir in the fish stock and cider. Return the pan to the heat and cook, stirring continuously, until the mixture comes to the boil and thickens.

Cook's tip This simple recipe can be adapted according to the varieties of fish and shellfish that are obtainable on the day – it is delicious whatever mixture you choose.

5 Add the potatoes. Bring the sauce back to the boil, then cover and simmer gently for 10–15 minutes until the potatoes are nearly tender.

6 Add all the fish and shellfish and stir in gently.

7 Stir in the cream. Bring back to a gentle simmer, then cover the pan and cook gently for 5–10 minutes or until the pieces of fish are cooked through and all the shells have opened. Adjust the seasoning to taste and gently stir in the herbs. Serve immediately.

Energy 583kcal/2439kJ; Protein 49.3g; Carbohydrate 25.3g, of which sugars 6.1g; Fat 30.2g, of which saturates 16.5g; Cholesterol 354mg; Calcium 199mg; Fibre 2.5g; Sodium 404mg

King scallops with bacon

This is a very simple yet luxurious dish, combining bacon and scallops with brown butter
which has just begun to burn. This gives the dish a lovely nutty smell, which is why the
French call this dish 'noisette' – nutty. Use hand-caught scallops if possible.

Serves 4

12 rashers (strips) streaky
(fatty) bacon

12 scallops

225g/8oz/1 cup unsalted butter

juice of 1 lemon

30ml/2 tbsp chopped fresh
flat leaf parsley

ground black pepper, to taste

1 Preheat the grill (broiler) to high.
Wrap a rasher of bacon around each
scallop so it goes over the top and not
round the side.

2 Cut the butter into chunks and put it
in a small pan over a low heat.

3 Meanwhile grill (broil) the scallops
with the bacon facing up so it protects
the meat. The bacon fat will help to
cook the scallops. This will take only a
few minutes; once they are cooked set
aside and keep warm.

4 Allow the butter to turn a nutty
brown colour, gently swirling it from
time to time. Just as it is foaming and
darkening, take off the heat and add
the lemon juice. Be warned, it will
bubble up quite dramatically.

5 Place the scallops on warmed plates,
dress with plenty of chopped fresh
parsley and pour the butter over.

Cook's Tip
Get the scallops on to warmed plates
just as the butter is coming to the right
colour, then add the lemon juice.

Energy 665kcal/2749kJ; Protein 24.4g; Carbohydrate 2.7g, of which sugars 0.6g; Fat 62g, of which saturates 34.7g; Cholesterol 189mg; Calcium 51mg; Fibre 0.5g; Sodium 1240mg

Oysters grilled with a herb and cheese crust

When buying oysters that are already shucked (opened and lifted from the shells), try and retain their juices so you can spoon some back into the shells for cooking. It is also nice to put a teaspoonful of laverbread in with each oyster before adding the breadcrumb topping.

Serves 2

6–8 oysters

½ lemon

sweet chilli sauce (optional)

50g/2oz/1 cup fresh breadcrumbs

50g/2oz/½ cup grated hard cheese

15ml/1 tbsp finely chopped chives

15ml/1 tbsp finely chopped parsley

salt and ground black pepper

50g/2oz/¼ cup butter

1 Scrub and open the oysters. Lay them, in the deep shells, in a grill (broiler) pan and squeeze a little lemon juice on to each one. Add a tiny drop of chilli sauce to each shell, if using.

2 Preheat the grill (broiler). Mix the breadcrumbs with the cheese, herbs, and a little seasoning. Spoon the mixture on top of the oysters and dot with tiny pieces of butter.

3 Cook under the grill (not too close) for about 5 minutes, or until the topping is crisp golden brown and bubbling around the edges.

Cook's tip
To open a live oyster, hold it in a cloth firmly with one hand and, with a special pointed knife, prize open at the hinge.

Energy 433kcal/1804kJ; Protein 18.3g; Carbohydrate 21.9g, of which sugars 1g; Fat 30.4g, of which saturates 18.6g; Cholesterol 123mg; Calcium 349mg; Fibre 1g; Sodium 933mg

Mussels in cider

There are numerous recipes for mussels around Britain. Here they are cooked simply and quickly with a delicious broth of cider, garlic and cream. Serve in large shallow bowls with a chunk of bread to mop up the juices and a glass of local cider.

2 Melt the butter gently in a very large pan and add the leek and garlic. Cook over medium heat for about 5 minutes, stirring frequently, until the vegetables are very soft but not browned. Season with pepper.

3 Add the cider and immediately tip in the mussels. Cover with a lid and cook quickly, shaking the pan occasionally, until the mussels have just opened (take care not to overcook and toughen them).

4 Remove the lid, add the cream and parsley and bubble gently for a minute or two. Serve immediately in shallow bowls.

**Serves 4 as an appetizer,
2 as a main course**

1.8kg/4lb mussels in their shells

40g/1½oz/3 tbsp butter

1 leek, washed and finely chopped

1 garlic clove, finely chopped

ground black pepper

150ml/¼ pint/⅔ cup dry (hard) cider

30–45ml/2–3 tbsp double (heavy) cream

a handful of fresh parsley, chopped

1 Scrub the mussels and scrape off any barnacles. Discard those with broken shells or that refuse to close when given a sharp tap with a knife. Pull off the hairy beards with a sharp tug.

Cook's tip
Eat mussels the fun way! Use an empty shell as pincers to pick out the mussels from the other shells. Don't try to eat any whose shells have not opened during cooking.

Energy 261kcal/1092kJ; Protein 21.1g; Carbohydrate 6.5g, of which sugars 2.1g; Fat 15.6g, of which saturates 8.2g; Cholesterol 104mg; Calcium 82mg; Fibre 1g; Sodium 498mg

Cockle cakes

One of the simplest ways to serve cockles is to toss them in fine oatmeal and briefly fry them. Here, they are made into cakes, nicest when cooked in bacon fat, though you could of course simply fry them in oil or butter. They are particularly good served with eggs.

Makes 4-8

125g/4½oz/1 cup plain
(all-purpose) flour

1 egg

150ml/¼ pint/⅔ cup milk

ground black pepper

100g/3¾oz shelled cooked cockles
(small clams)

15–30ml/1–2 tbsp chopped fresh
chives (optional)

6 bacon rashers (slices)

vegetable oil for frying

1 Sift the flour into a bowl, make a well in the centre and break the egg into it.

2 Mix the egg into the flour, gradually stirring in the milk to make a smooth batter. Season with pepper and stir in the cockles and chives (if using).

3 Heat a little oil in a pan, add the bacon and fry quickly. Lift out and keep warm.

4 Add tablespoonfuls of batter to the hot bacon fat, leaving them space to spread. Cook until crisp and golden, turning over once. Drain and serve with the bacon.

Energy 137kcal/572kJ; Protein 7g; Carbohydrate 13.1g, of which sugars 1.2g; Fat 6.6g, of which saturates 1.7g; Cholesterol 40mg; Calcium 63mg; Fibre 0.5g; Sodium 322mg

Poultry, meat and game

The British diet has always relied on plentiful supplies of meat. In past times, most families fattened up a pig in the garden, cured their own bacon and kept a few hens, ducks and geese, and these formed the basis of the many classics that are still around today. From the traditional Sunday roast to hearty casseroles, thick broths, pastries, pies and pan-fried dishes, there is a huge range of poultry and meat dishes to choose from, whatever the occasion.

Stoved chicken

The word 'stoved' is derived from the French *étuver* – to cook in a covered pot – and originates from the time of the Franco-Scottish Alliance in the 17th century. Instead of buying chicken joints, you could use either chicken thighs or chicken drumsticks.

Serves 4

900g/2lb potatoes, cut into 5mm/¼in slices

2 large onions, thinly sliced

15ml/1 tbsp chopped fresh thyme

salt and ground black pepper

25g/1oz/¼ stick butter

15ml/1 tbsp vegetable oil

2 large bacon rashers (strips), chopped

4 large chicken joints, halved

1 bay leaf

600ml/1 pint/2½ cups chicken stock

1 Preheat the oven to 150°C/300°F/ Gas 2. Make a thick layer of half the potato slices in the base of a large, heavy casserole, then cover with half the onion. Sprinkle with half the thyme and salt and ground black pepper.

2 Heat the butter and oil in a large frying pan then brown the bacon and chicken. Using a slotted spoon, transfer the chicken and bacon to the casserole. Reserve the fat in the pan.

3 Tuck the bay leaf in between the chicken. Sprinkle the remaining thyme over, then cover with the remaining onion, followed by a neat layer of overlapping potato slices. Season.

4 Pour the stock into the casserole. Brush the top layer of the sliced potatoes with the reserved fat from the frying pan, then cover tightly and cook in the preheated oven for about 2 hours, until the chicken is thoroughly cooked and tender.

5 Preheat the grill (broiler) to high. Uncover the casserole and place under the grill and cook until the slices of potato are beginning to brown and crisp. Serve hot.

Variation
You can use tarragon instead of the thyme: French tarragon has a superior flavour to the Russian variety.

Energy 630kcal/2653kJ; Protein 69.2g; Carbohydrate 48.2g, of which sugars 8.9g; Fat 19.2g, of which saturates 7.2g; Cholesterol 195mg; Calcium 57mg; Fibre 3.9g; Sodium 574mg

Roast chicken with leek, laver and lemon stuffing

The three 'Ls' – leek, laver and lemon – commonly used in Welsh cooking complement each other beautifully to make a light and unusual stuffing that goes perfectly with chicken. You can also add finely grated cheese to the mixture, if you like.

Serves 4–6

1.4–1.8kg/3–4lb oven-ready chicken

1 small onion, quartered

½ lemon, roughly chopped

2 garlic cloves, halved

olive oil or melted butter

For the stuffing

30ml/2 tbsp olive oil

2 rindless bacon rashers (slices), finely chopped

1 small leek, thinly sliced

1 garlic clove, crushed or finely chopped

30ml/2 tbsp laverbread

150g/5oz/1¼ cups fresh breadcrumbs

finely grated rind and juice of ½ lemon

salt and ground black pepper

1 To make the stuffing, put the oil and bacon into a pan and cook over medium heat, stirring occasionally, for about 3 minutes without browning. Add the leek and garlic and cook for 3–5 minutes, stirring occasionally, until soft and just beginning to brown. Remove from the heat and stir in the laverbread, breadcrumbs, lemon rind and juice, and seasoning. Leave to cool.

Cook's tip

The stuffing is also excellent for spooning under the skin of chicken breasts, or piling on to fillets of fish before oven cooking.

2 Preheat the oven to 200°C/400°F/Gas 6. Rinse the chicken inside and out, and then pat dry with kitchen paper. Spoon the cooled stuffing into the neck cavity of the chicken and fold the skin over and under. Any excess stuffing can be put under the breast skin – loosen it carefully by sliding your fingers underneath and then fill the resulting pocket evenly.

3 Put the onion, lemon and garlic into the main cavity of the chicken. Sit the bird in a roasting tin (pan) and brush it all over with olive oil or melted butter. Cover the breast area with a small piece of foil.

4 Put into the hot oven and cook for about 1½ hours, or until the chicken is cooked through (when a sharp knife is inserted in the thick part of the thigh next to the breast, the juices should run clear, not pink). Remove the foil for the final 30 minutes of cooking to allow the skin to brown and crisp.

5 Remove from the oven and leave to rest in a warm place for 15–20 minutes before carving. Reheat the pan juices and serve them spooned over the chicken.

Energy 486kcal/2027kJ; Protein 33.4g; Carbohydrate 22.3g, of which sugars 1.2g; Fat 29.7g, of which saturates 8.1g; Cholesterol 154mg; Calcium 54mg; Fibre 1g; Sodium 461mg

Michaelmas goose with apple stuffing

This hearty recipe includes apples, at their best in autumn and a refreshing foil to the richness of the goose and the traditional black pudding. Serve the goose with roast potatoes, seasonal vegetables and apple sauce or bramble jelly.

Serves 6–8

1 goose, 4.5kg/10lb, with giblets

1 onion, sliced

2 carrots, sliced

2 celery sticks, sliced

a small bunch of parsley and thyme

salt and ground black pepper

450g/1lb black pudding (blood sausage), crumbled or chopped

2 large cooking apples, peeled, cored and finely chopped

1 large garlic clove, crushed

250ml/8fl oz/1 cup dry (hard) cider

15ml/1 tbsp plain (all-purpose) flour

watercress or parsley, to garnish

1 Remove the goose liver from the giblets and put the remainder into a pan with the onion, carrots, celery and herbs. Cover with cold water, season and simmer for 30–45 minutes to make a stock for the gravy. Preheat the oven to 200°C/400°F/Gas 6.

2 Meanwhile, chop the liver and mix it with the black pudding, garlic and apples. Season, then sprinkle in 75ml/ 2½fl oz/⅓ cup cider to bind.

3 Wipe out the goose and stuff it with this mixture, being careful not to pack it too tightly. Prick the skin all over with a fork, sprinkle generously with salt and pepper and rub in well.

4 Weigh the stuffed goose and calculate the cooking time at 15 minutes per 450g/1lb, plus 15 minutes over. Put on a rack in a large roasting pan, cover with foil and put it into the preheated oven.

5 After 1 hour, remove the goose from the oven and carefully pour off the hot fat that has accumulated in the bottom of the pan; reserve this fat for cooking. Pour the remaining dry cider over the goose and return to the oven.

6 Half an hour before the end of the cooking time, remove the foil and baste the goose with the juices.

7 Return to the oven, uncovered, and allow to brown, basting occasionally. When cooked, transfer to a heated serving dish. Put it in a warm place to rest.

8 Meanwhile, make the gravy. Pour off any excess fat from the roasting pan, leaving 30ml/2 tbsp, then sprinkle in enough flour to absorb it. Cook over a medium heat for a minute, scraping the pan to loosen the sediment. Strain the giblet stock and stir in enough to make the gravy. Bring to the boil and simmer for a few minutes, stirring constantly. Add any juices that have accumulated under the goose, season to taste and pour the gravy into a heated sauceboat.

9 Garnish the goose with the parsley or watercress. Carve into slices at the table and serve with the gravy, roast potatoes and some seasonal vegetables.

Energy 795kcal/3297kJ; Protein 32.8g; Carbohydrate 17.1g, of which sugars 2.3g; Fat 65.4g, of which saturates 20.6g; Cholesterol 171mg; Calcium 109mg; Fibre 0.4g; Sodium 800mg

Rabbit with apricots

Rabbit is a delicious meat, richer and more tasty than chicken, but with a similar colouring and texture. The gamey flavours go very well in many dishes, especially those with fruits and berries. Once a staple of the countryside, it is now available from some butchers.

Serves 4

2 rabbits

30ml/2 tbsp plain (all-purpose) flour

salt and ground black pepper

15ml/1 tbsp vegetable oil

90g/3½oz streaky (fatty) bacon, cut into thin pieces

10 baby (pearl) onions, peeled but kept whole

200ml/7fl oz/scant 1 cup dry white wine

1 bay leaf

12 dried apricots

Cook's Tip
This dish is best reheated until piping hot and served the next day so that the flavours can develop overnight.

1 Ask your butcher to joint the rabbits, providing two legs and the saddle cut in two.

2 Sprinkle the flour over a dish, season with salt and ground black pepper and mix well into the flour. Roll the rabbit pieces in it one by one to coat lightly all over, shaking off any excess flour. Set aside.

3 Heat a heavy pan and add the oil. Brown the rabbit pieces all over then remove from the pan. Brown the bacon followed by the onions.

4 Place the browned rabbit pieces, bacon and onions in a casserole. Pour the wine into the heavy pan and, over a low heat, scrape up all the bits from the base of the pan.

5 Add a little water, bring to the boil and pour over the rabbit in the casserole, adding water to just cover.

6 Add the bay leaf and bring to the boil. Allow to simmer gently for 40 minutes until the rabbit is tender.

7 Remove the rabbit and onions from the pan and set aside, keeping them warm. Put the apricots into the pan and boil rapidly until the cooking liquor thickens slightly. Remove the bay leaf and check the seasoning.

8 You can now either return the rabbit and onions to the pan as it is and heat before serving, or you can purée the apricots in the cooking liquor and pour the resulting rich sauce over the rabbit.

Energy 481kcal/2022kJ; Protein 60.2g; Carbohydrate 22.5g, of which sugars 21.4g; Fat 13.8g, of which saturates 6.1g; Cholesterol 223mg; Calcium 153mg; Fibre 3.9g; Sodium 417mg

Spiced pork roast with apple and thyme cream sauce

Belly of pork (sometimes called 'lap' of pork) makes a tasty and tender roasting joint. In this satisfying, warming dish, the pork is boned and skinned for stuffing and rolling. Serve with mashed potato, carrots and sprouting broccoli.

Serves 6

1 medium onion, finely chopped

3 garlic cloves, crushed

75g/3oz/6 tbsp butter

bunch of mixed fresh herbs, leaves finely chopped

225g/8oz/4 cups fine fresh breadcrumbs

1 egg, beaten

salt and ground black pepper

1 piece of pork belly, about 1.3kg/3lb

15ml/1 tbsp vegetable oil

For the spicy paste

25g/1oz/2 tbsp butter, melted

30ml/2 tbsp chutney

15ml/1 tbsp lemon juice

2 garlic cloves, crushed

30ml/2 tbsp mild mustard, with Guinness or whiskey, if available

For the sauce

2 large cooking apples, peeled, cored and chopped

1 medium onion, chopped

2 garlic cloves, crushed

1 or 2 thyme sprigs

150ml/¼ pint/⅔ cup medium (hard) cider

150ml/¼ pint/⅔ cup chicken stock

300ml/½ pint/1¼ cups single (light) cream

1 Cook the onion and garlic in the butter until soft, then add the herbs and breadcrumbs. Cool a little before mixing in the egg, and season well with salt and ground pepper. Preheat the oven to 150°C/300°F/Gas 2.

2 Meanwhile, trim off any fat from the meat and prick the centre with a fork; combine all the spicy paste ingredients together and brush the meat with some of it. Spread the stuffing over the meat, then roll it up and tie with cook's string.

3 Brown the meat in the oil in a hot roasting pan, then transfer to the oven and roast for 3 hours. Halfway through cooking remove the joint from the oven and brush liberally with more spicy paste; turn over and return to the oven.

4 To make the thyme cream sauce, put the cooking apples, onion and garlic in a large pan and add the thyme sprigs, cider and stock. Bring to the boil and simmer gently for 15 minutes, then discard the thyme. Add the cream. Process the mixture in a blender, strain and season to taste with salt and black pepper. If the sauce seems too thick, adjust the texture with extra stock.

5 Serve the sliced meat on heated plates with the sauce.

Left *Apple trees in blossom on a fruit farm in County Armagh.*

Energy 814kcal/3409kJ; Protein 73.2g; Carbohydrate 41.9g, of which sugars 12.6g; Fat 39.8g, of which saturates 20.2g; Cholesterol 264mg; Calcium 145mg; Fibre 2.4g; Sodium 581mg

Bacon chops with apple and cider sauce

Either thick bacon or pork chops could be used in this recipe, which brings classic ingredients together in an attractive modern British dish. Serve with lots of creamy mashed potatoes and steamed buttered cabbage for a tasty, warming meal.

Serves 4

15ml/1 tbsp vegetable oil

4 bacon chops

1 or 2 cooking apples

knob (pat) of butter

1 or 2 garlic cloves, finely chopped

5ml/1 tsp sugar

150ml/¼ pint/⅔ cup dry (hard) cider

5ml/1 tsp cider vinegar

15ml/1 tbsp wholegrain mustard

10ml/2 tsp chopped fresh thyme

salt and ground black pepper

sprigs of thyme, to garnish

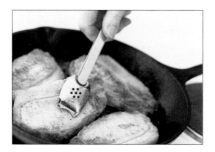

1 Heat the oil in a large heavy frying pan, over a medium heat, and cook the chops for 10–15 minutes, browning well on both sides.

2 Peel, core and slice the apples. Remove the chops from the pan and keep warm. Add the butter and apples to the pan and cook until the juices begin to brown.

3 Add the finely chopped garlic and sugar, and cook for 1 minute, then stir in the cider, cider vinegar, mustard and chopped thyme. Boil for a few minutes until reduced to a saucy consistency.

4 Season the sauce. Place the chops on warmed serving plates and pour over the sauce. Garnish with the thyme sprigs.

Energy 285kcal/1190kJ; Protein 26.4g; Carbohydrate 6.5g, of which sugars 6.5g; Fat 16.1g, of which saturates 5.4g; Cholesterol 40mg; Calcium 17mg; Fibre 0.8g; Sodium 1340mg

Braised sausages with onions, celeriac and apple

Britain boasts a wealth of wonderful sausages made by artisan producers across the regions. For this recipe, choose your favourite good-quality sausages, such as traditional pork, Cumberland, or something more unusual, such as duck, venison or wild boar.

Serves 4

30ml/2 tbsp vegetable oil

8 meaty sausages

2 onions, sliced

15ml/1 tbsp plain (all-purpose) flour

400ml/14fl oz/1⅔ cups dry (hard) cider

350g/12oz celeriac, cut into chunks

15ml/1 tbsp Worcestershire sauce

15ml/1 tbsp chopped fresh sage

salt and ground black pepper

2 small cooking apples

1 Preheat the oven to 180°C/350°F/ Gas 4. Heat the oil in a frying pan, add the sausages and fry for about 5 minutes until evenly browned.

2 Transfer the sausages to an ovenproof casserole dish and drain any excess oil from the pan to leave 15ml/1 tbsp. Add the onions and cook for a few minutes, stirring occasionally, until softened and turning golden.

3 Stir in the flour, then gradually add the cider and bring to the boil, stirring. Add the celeriac and stir in the Worcestershire sauce and sage. Season with salt and black pepper.

4 Pour the cider and celeriac mixture over the sausages. Cover, put into the hot oven and cook for 30 minutes, or until the celeriac is soft.

5 Quarter the apples, remove their cores and cut into thick slices. Stir the apple slices into the casserole, cover and cook for a further 10–15 minutes, or until the apples are just tender. Taste and adjust the seasoning if necessary before serving.

Energy 508kcal/2114kJ; Protein 12.7g; Carbohydrate 29.3g, of which sugars 13.6g; Fat 35.8g, of which saturates 12.3g; Cholesterol 45mg; Calcium 131mg; Fibre 3.3g; Sodium 1019mg

Lancashire hotpot

This famous hotpot was traditionally cooked in a farmhouse or communal bread oven, in time for supper at the end of the day. The ingredients would have been layered straight into the pot, but here the meat is first browned to add colour and extra flavour to the dish.

Serves 4

15–30ml/1–2 tbsp vegetable oil

8–12 lean best end of neck (cross rib) lamb chops

about 175g/6oz lamb's kidneys, skin and core removed and cut into pieces

2 medium onions, thinly sliced

few sprigs of fresh thyme or rosemary

900g/2lb potatoes, thinly sliced

600ml/1 pint/2½ cups lamb or vegetable stock

25g/1oz/2 tbsp butter, in small pieces

salt and ground black pepper

1 Preheat the oven to 180°C/350°F/ Gas 4. Heat the oil in a large frying pan and brown the lamb chops quickly on all sides. Remove the meat from the pan and set aside.

Variation Add sliced carrots or mushrooms to the layers. Replace 150ml/¼ pint/⅔ cup of the stock with dry (hard) cider or wine.

2 Add the kidney to the hot pan and brown lightly over a high heat. Lift out.

3 In a casserole, layer the chops and kidneys with the onions, herbs and potatoes, seasoning each layer.

4 Finish off with a layer of potatoes. Pour over the stock, sprinkle with herbs and dot the top with butter. Cover, put into the oven and cook for 2 hours. Remove the lid, increase the temperature to 220°C/425°F/Gas 7 and cook, uncovered, for 30 minutes more until the potatoes are crisp. Serve hot.

Energy 810kcal/3400kJ; Protein 76.7g; Carbohydrate 43.7g, of which sugars 9.3g; Fat 37.8g, of which saturates 13.2g; Cholesterol 363mg; Calcium 140mg; Fibre 6.2g; Sodium 285mg

Roast shoulder of lamb with mint sauce

Lamb is one of the three meats (with beef and pork) that is traditionally roasted and served for Sunday lunch. It is particularly popular at Easter. Mint sauce, with its sweet-sour combination, has been lamb's customary accompaniment since at least the 17th century.

Serves 6–8

For the mint sauce

large handful of fresh mint leaves

15ml/1 tbsp caster (superfine) sugar

45–60ml/3–4 tbsp cider vinegar or wine vinegar

boned shoulder of lamb, weighing 1.5–2kg/3¼–4½lb

30ml/2 tbsp fresh thyme leaves

30ml/2 tbsp clear honey

150ml/¼ pint/⅔ cup dry (hard) cider or white wine

30–45ml/2–3 tbsp double (heavy) cream (optional)

salt and ground black pepper

1 Preheat the oven to 220°C/425°F/ Gas 7. To make the mint sauce, finely chop the mint leaves with the sugar (the sugar draws the juices from the mint) and put the mixture into a bowl.

2 Add 30ml/2 tbsp boiling water (from the kettle) to the mint and sugar, and stir well until the sugar has dissolved. Add the vinegar to taste and leave the sauce to stand for at least 1 hour for the flavours to blend.

3 Open out the lamb with skin side down. Season with salt and pepper, sprinkle with the thyme leaves and drizzle the honey over the top. Roll up and tie securely with string in several places. Place the meat in a roasting pan and put into the hot oven. Cook for 30 minutes until browned all over.

4 Pour the cider and 150ml/¼ pint/ ⅔ cup water into the tin. Lower the oven to 160°C/325°F/Gas 3 and cook for about 45 minutes for medium (pink) or about 1 hour for well-done meat.

5 Remove the lamb from the oven, cover loosely with a sheet of foil and leave to stand for 20–30 minutes.

6 Lift the lamb on to a warmed serving plate. Skim any excess fat from the surface of the pan juices before reheating and seasoning to taste. Stir in the cream, if using, bring to the boil and remove from the heat. Carve the lamb and serve it with the pan juices spooned over and the mint sauce.

Energy 351kcal/1468kJ; Protein 36.9g; Carbohydrate 2.5g, of which sugars 2.5g; Fat 21g, of which saturates 9.8g; Cholesterol 143mg; Calcium 23mg; Fibre 0g; Sodium 202mg

Beef Wellington

This dish is derived from the classic French *boeuf en croûte*. The English name was applied to it in honour of the Duke of Wellington, following his victory at the Battle of Waterloo in 1815. Begin preparing the dish in advance to allow the meat to cool before it is wrapped in pastry.

2 Heat the remaining oil and cook the mushrooms and garlic for 5 minutes, until softened. Beat the mushrooms into the pâté. Add the parsley, season and leave to cool.

3 Roll out the pastry, reserving a small amount, into a rectangle large enough to enclose the beef. Spread the pâté mixture down the middle, untie the beef and lay it on the pâté.

Serves 6

1.5kg/3lb 6oz fillet of beef

45ml/3 tbsp vegetable oil

115g/4oz mushrooms, chopped

2 garlic cloves, crushed

175g/6oz smooth liver pâté

30ml/2 tbsp chopped fresh parsley

salt and ground black pepper

400g/14oz puff pastry

beaten egg, to glaze

1 Tie the fillet at intervals with string. Heat 30ml/2 tbsp of the oil, and brown on all sides over a high heat. Transfer to a roasting pan and cook in the oven for 20 minutes. Leave to cool.

4 Preheat the oven to 220°C/425°F/ Gas 7. Brush the pastry edges with beaten egg and fold it over the meat. Place, seam down, on a baking sheet. Cut leaves from the reserved pastry and decorate the top. Brush the parcel with beaten egg. Chill for 10 minutes or until the oven is hot.

5 Cook for 50–60 minutes, covering loosely with foil after about 30 minutes to prevent the pastry burning. Cut into thick slices to serve.

Energy 511kcal/2131kJ; Protein 41.7g; Carbohydrate 19.3g, of which sugars 1.2g; Fat 30.6g, of which saturates 7.2g; Cholesterol 128mg; Calcium 41mg; Fibre 0.4g; Sodium 320mg

Cornish pasties

The original portable lunch, pasties made a satisfying midday meal for intrepid Cornish tin miners, who could use the crimped pastry join across the top as a handle if their hands were filthy. These contain the traditional filling of chopped steak and root vegetables.

Makes 6

500–675g/1¼–1½lb shortcrust pastry

450g/1lb chuck steak, cubed

1 potato, about 175g/6oz, cubed

175g/6oz swede (rutabaga), cubed

1 onion, finely chopped

2.5ml/½ tsp dried mixed herbs

salt and ground black pepper

beaten egg, to glaze

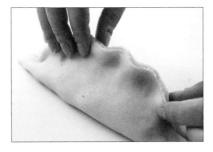

3 Brush the edges with water, then fold the pastry over the filling. Crimp the edges firmly together.

4 Use a fish slice to transfer the pasties to a non-stick baking sheet, then brush each one with beaten egg.

5 Put into the hot oven and cook for 15 minutes, then reduce the oven temperature to 160°C/325°F/Gas 3 and cook for a further 1 hour.

Cook's tip Swede (rutabaga) is the traditional vegetable in Cornish pasties, but turnip, carrot or celery could be used in its place, if you prefer.

1 Preheat the oven to 220°C/425°F/Gas 7. Divide the pastry into six equal pieces, then roll out each piece to form a rough circle, measuring about 20cm/8in.

2 Mix together the steak, vegetables, herbs and seasoning, then spoon an equal amount on to one half of each pastry circle.

Energy 414kcal/1731kJ; Protein 10.4g; Carbohydrate 38.8g, of which sugars 1.4g; Fat 25.3g, of which saturates 9.2g; Cholesterol 51mg; Calcium 93mg; Fibre 1.4g; Sodium 620mg

Veal and ham pie

In the cold version of veal and ham pie, the filling is completely enclosed in hot water crust pastry. In this hot version, the pastry sits on top of the classic combination of meat and eggs, keeping the contents moist and the aromas sealed in until the pie is cut open.

Serves 4

450g/1lb boneless shoulder of veal, cut into cubes

225g/8oz lean gammon, cut into cubes

15ml/1 tbsp plain (all-purpose) flour

large pinch each of dry mustard and ground black pepper

25g/1oz/2 tbsp butter

15ml/1 tbsp vegetable oil

1 onion, chopped

600ml/1 pint/2½ cups chicken or veal stock

2 eggs, hard-boiled and sliced

30ml/2 tbsp chopped fresh parsley

For the pastry

175g/6oz/1½ cups plain (all-purpose) flour

pinch of salt

85g/3oz/6 tbsp butter, diced

beaten egg, to glaze

1 Preheat the oven to 180°C/350°F/ Gas 4. Mix the veal and gammon in a bowl. Season the flour with the mustard and black pepper, then add it to the meat and toss well.

2 Heat the butter and oil in a large, flameproof casserole until sizzling, then cook the meat mixture in batches until golden on all sides. Use a slotted spoon to remove the meat and set aside.

3 Cook the onion in the fat remaining in the casserole until softened but not coloured. Stir in the meat and the stock. Cover and cook in the hot oven for 1½ hours or until the veal is tender. Adjust the seasoning and leave to cool.

4 To make the pastry, sift the flour into a large bowl with the salt and rub in the butter until the mixture resembles fine crumbs. Mix in just enough cold water to bind the mixture, gathering it together with your fingertips. Wrap the pastry in clear film (plastic wrap), and chill in the refrigerator for at least 30 minutes.

Variation Use ready-made fresh or frozen puff pastry to cover the pie.

5 Spoon the veal mixture into a 1.5 litre/ 2½ pint/6¼ cup pie dish. Arrange the slices of hard-boiled egg on top and sprinkle with the parsley.

6 On a lightly floured surface, roll out the pastry to about 4cm/1½in larger than the top of the pie dish. Cut a strip from around the edge, dampen the rim of the dish and press the pastry strip on to it. Brush the pastry rim with beaten egg and top with the lid.

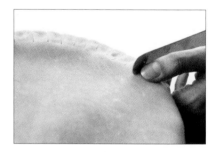

7 Trim off any excess pastry. Use the blunt edge of a knife to tap the outside edge, pressing the pastry down with your finger to seal in the filling. Pinch the pastry between your fingers to flute the edge. Roll out any trimmings and cut out shapes to decorate the pie.

8 Brush the top of the pie with beaten egg, put into the hot oven and cook for 30–40 minutes or until the pastry is well risen and golden brown. Serve hot.

Energy 621kcal/2595kJ; Protein 42.4g; Carbohydrate 39.2g, of which sugars 2.6g; Fat 33.8g, of which saturates 17.2g; Cholesterol 281mg; Calcium 128mg; Fibre 2.3g; Sodium 1007mg

Venison stew

This simple yet deeply flavoured stew makes a wonderful supper dish, incorporating rich red wine and sweet redcurrant jelly with the depth of the bacon. Venison is popular in Scotland but you could substitute good-quality beef, if you prefer. It is a very lean meat, so bacon is included in this dish to provide some fat for the sauce.

Serves 4

1.3kg/3lb stewing venison (shoulder or topside), trimmed

50g/2oz/¼ cup butter

225g/8oz piece of streaky (fatty) bacon, cut into 2cm/¾in lardons

2 large onions, chopped

1 large carrot, peeled and diced

1 large garlic clove, crushed

30ml/2 tbsp plain (all-purpose) flour

½ bottle red wine

beef stock (see Step 4)

1 bay leaf

sprig of fresh thyme

200g/7oz button (white) mushrooms, sliced

30ml/2 tbsp redcurrant jelly

salt and ground black pepper

1 Cut the venison into cubes, then dry it thoroughly using kitchen paper. Set to one side.

2 Melt the butter in a large, heavy pan then brown the bacon over a medium-high heat, stirring occasionally. Reduce the heat to medium and add the onions and carrot, stir in and brown lightly.

3 Add the venison to the pan along with the garlic and stir into the mixture. Sprinkle on the flour and mix well.

4 Add the wine and enough stock to cover, along with the herbs, mushrooms redcurrant jelly and seasoning.

5 Cover the pan and simmer over a low heat until the meat is cooked, approximately 1½–2 hours. Serve immediately with creamy mashed potato and green vegetables of your choice.

Energy 727kcal/3045kJ; Protein 83.8g; Carbohydrate 17.5g, of which sugars 14.4g; Fat 31.3g, of which saturates 13.8g; Cholesterol 226mg; Calcium 70mg; Fibre 2.9g; Sodium 985mg

Rissoles

In a 16th-century English recipe for 'rissheshewes', finely chopped cooked meat was mixed with breadcrumbs and bound into little cakes with beaten eggs and a thick gravy. These contemporary rissoles have been adapted to feature mashed potato, which makes the mixture easier to shape and coat with crumbs.

Serves 4

675g/1½lb potatoes, peeled

350g/12oz cooked beef or lamb, such as the remains of a joint, trimmed of excess fat

1 small onion

5ml/1 tsp Worcestershire sauce

30ml/2 tbsp chopped fresh herbs, such as parsley, mint and chives

salt and ground black pepper

30ml/2 tbsp plain (all-purpose) flour

2 eggs, beaten

115g/4oz/2 cups fresh breadcrumbs

vegetable oil for frying

brown sauce, to serve

1 Cook the whole potatoes in boiling water for about 20 minutes or until completely soft. Meanwhile, mince (grind) or chop the meat very finely. Finely chop the onion.

2 Drain the potatoes and mash them thoroughly by pushing the warm potatoes through a ricer, passing them through a mouli, or mashing them with a potato masher or fork.

3 In a large mixing bowl combine the meat and onion with the potatoes, Worcestershire sauce, herbs and seasoning, beating well. Shape the mixture into eight patties or sausages.

Cook's tip Chilling the potato and meat mixture before shaping the rissoles will make it easier to handle.

4 Dip in the flour, then in the beaten egg and finally in the breadcrumbs, gently shaking off any excess.

5 Heat enough oil to cover the base of a large frying pan and cook the rissoles over a medium heat, turning once or twice, until crisp and golden brown. Drain and serve with brown sauce.

Energy 519kcal/2184kJ; Protein 27.4g; Carbohydrate 56.7g, of which sugars 4.1g; Fat 22g, of which saturates 6.5g; Cholesterol 162mg; Calcium 86mg; Fibre 2.8g; Sodium 363mg

Liver, bacon and onions

Simple yet so full of flavour, this dish was traditionally made with pig's liver. Nowadays lamb's liver is more popular, but you can use pig's liver if you prefer – although it has a much stronger flavour. Serve with creamy mashed potatoes to soak up the sauce, maybe with swede, parsnip or pumpkin added. Don't overcook the liver, as it will toughen.

Serves 4

450g/1lb lamb's liver

30ml/2 tbsp plain (all-purpose) flour

salt and ground black pepper

15ml/1 tbsp vegetable oil, plus extra if necessary

8 rindless streaky (fatty) bacon rashers (slices)

2 onions, thinly sliced

4 fresh small sage leaves, chopped

150ml/¼ pint/⅔ cup chicken stock

1 Pat the liver with kitchen paper, then trim it and, with a sharp knife, cut on the diagonal to make thick strips. Season the flour and toss the liver in it until it is well coated, shaking off any excess flour.

2 Heat the oil in a large frying pan and add the bacon. Cook over medium heat until the fat runs out of the bacon and it is browned and crisp. Lift out and keep warm.

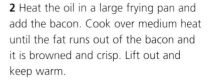

3 Add the onions and sage to the frying pan. Cook over medium heat for about 10–15 minutes, stirring occasionally, until the onions are soft and golden brown. Lift out with a slotted spoon and keep warm.

4 Increase the heat under the pan and, adding a little extra oil if necessary, add the liver in a single layer. Cook for 3–4 minutes, turning once, until browned on both sides.

5 Return the onions to the pan and pour in the stock. Bring just to the boil and bubble gently for a minute or two, seasoning to taste with salt and pepper. Serve topped with the bacon.

Energy 310kcal/1293kJ; Protein 28.7g; Carbohydrate 13.7g, of which sugars 5.7g; Fat 15.9g, of which saturates 4.4g; Cholesterol 500mg; Calcium 44mg; Fibre 1.6g; Sodium 400mg

Faggots with onion gravy

In the days when most households reared a pig at the bottom of the garden, these faggots were made with the fresh liver on slaughter day. The pâté-like mixture was wrapped in the lacy netting of the pig's caul, which held the contents together during the cooking process. In this recipe, beaten egg binds the mixture. Serve with peas.

Serves 4

450g/1lb pig's liver, trimmed and roughly chopped

300g/11oz belly pork, roughly chopped

2 onions, roughly chopped

100g/3¾oz/1 cup fresh breadcrumbs

1 egg, beaten

2 sage leaves, chopped

5ml/1 tsp salt

2.5ml/½ tsp ground mace

1.5ml/¼ tsp ground black pepper

150ml/¼ pint/⅔ cup beef or vegetable stock

butter, for greasing

For the onion gravy:

50g/2oz/¼ cup butter

4 onions (white, red or a mixture), thinly sliced

generous 10ml/2 tsp sugar

15ml/1 tbsp plain (all-purpose) flour

300ml/½ pint/1¼ cups good beef stock

300ml/½ pint/1¼ cups good vegetable stock

salt and black pepper

1 Preheat the oven to 180°C/350°F/Gas 4. Put the liver, pork and onions in a food processor and process until finely chopped. Turn the mixture out into a large mixing bowl and stir in the breadcrumbs, egg, sage, salt, mace and pepper until thoroughly combined.

2 With wet hands, shape the mixture into 10–12 round faggots and lay them in a shallow ovenproof dish. Add the stock.

3 Use a buttered sheet of foil to cover the dish, butter side down. Crimp the edges around the dish to seal them.

4 Cook in the oven for 45–50 minutes (the juices should run clear when the faggots are pierced with a sharp knife).

5 For the onion gravy, melt the butter in a large pan and add the onions and sugar. Cover and cook gently for at least 30 minutes, until the onions are soft and evenly caramelized to a rich golden brown.

6 Stir in the flour, remove from the heat and stir in both types of stock. Return the pan to the heat and, stirring continuously, bring just to the boil. Simmer gently for 20–30 minutes, stirring occasionally (if the liquid looks as if it's reducing too much, add a splash of water). Season to taste with salt and pepper.

7 Once the faggots are cooked, remove the foil covering them and increase the oven temperature to 200°C/400°F/Gas 6. Cook for 10 minutes more until lightly browned. Serve with the onion gravy.

Energy 664kcal/2768kJ; Protein 41.4g; Carbohydrate 31.2g, of which sugars 9.8g; Fat 42.5g, of which saturates 17.9g; Cholesterol 421mg; Calcium 84mg; Fibre 2.2g; Sodium 434mg

Side dishes

Almost as tasty as the main course itself, the
vegetables and salads in British cuisine provide a
fresh, often colourful accompaniment to every meal.
The richly flavoured green vegetables, including kale,
chard, spinach and cabbage, are excellent served on
their own or with a sauce. No meal is complete,
however, without those robust root vegetables:
turnip, swede, parsnip, carrot and – the versatile
favourite – the potato.

Mashed potatoes

The potato arrived in Britain in the latter half of the 16th century and at first was treated with great caution. Today, the British love them cooked in all kinds of ways. Fluffy mashed potatoes are the traditional accompaniment to sausages – or 'bangers'.

Serves 4

1kg/2¼lb floury potatoes, such as Maris Piper

about 150ml/¼pint/⅔ cup milk

115g/4oz/½ cup soft butter

salt

freshly grated nutmeg (optional)

1 Peel the potatoes and cook them whole in a large pan of boiling water for about 20 minutes or until soft throughout. Drain. Warm the milk and butter in a large pan.

2 Push the warm potatoes through a ricer, pass them through a mouli, or mash with a potato masher or fork.

3 Add the mashed potato to the milk and beat with a wooden spoon, adding extra milk if necessary to achieve the desired consistency. Season to taste with salt and a little nutmeg (if using).

Variations Cook a small onion, quartered, with the potatoes and mash it with them, or add a spoonful of English (hot) mustard or horseradish sauce to the mash.

Roast potatoes

Roast potatoes can be cooked around a joint of meat, where they will absorb the juices. For crisp potatoes with a soft, fluffy interior, roast them in a separate dish in a single layer.

Serves 4

1.3kg/3lb floury potatoes

90ml/6 tbsp vegetable oil, lard or goose fat

salt

1 Preheat the oven to 200°C/400°F/ Gas 6. Peel the potatoes and cut into chunks. Boil in salted water for about 5 minutes, drain, return to the pan, and shake them to roughen the surfaces.

2 Put the fat into a large roasting pan and put into the hot oven to heat it. Add the potatoes, coating them in the fat. Return to the oven and cook for 40–50 minutes, turning once or twice, until crisp and cooked through.

Energy 338kcal/1424kJ; Protein 5.9g; Carbohydrate 50.4g, of which sugars 3.3g; Fat 14g, of which saturates 9.1g; Cholesterol 39mg; Calcium 42mg; Fibre 3.6g; Sodium 140mg

Energy 484kcal/2048kJ; Protein 9.4g; Carbohydrate 84.2g, of which sugars 2g; Fat 14.6g, of which saturates 5.9g; Cholesterol 13mg; Calcium 26mg; Fibre 5.9g; Sodium 29mg

Chips

In 20th-century England, serving chips with fried fish developed into a national institution with the rise of the fish and chip shop. It was not long before chips were fried at home – once to cook them and the second time to brown and crisp them.

Serves 4

sunflower or vegetable oil, for deep-frying

675g/1½lb potatoes

salt

1 Heat the oil to 150°C/300°F. Peel the potatoes and cut them into chips about 1cm/½in thick. Rinse and dry.

2 Lower a batch of chips into the hot oil and cook for about 5 minutes or until tender but not browned. Lift out on to kitchen paper and leave to cool.

3 Just before serving, increase the temperature of the oil to 190°C/375°F. Add the par-cooked chips, in batches.

4 Cook until crisp, then lift out and drain on kitchen paper. Sprinkle with salt and serve at once.

Baked jacket potatoes

When the potato, one of Britain's staple foods, is cooked in its 'jacket' (skin) in the oven it can be served split and laced with butter or sour cream, or with a filling of grated cheese.

Serves 4

4 large floury potatoes of even size, such as King Edward or Maris Piper

a little vegetable oil

salt (optional)

butter or sour cream, to serve

chopped fresh parsley or chives, to serve

1 Preheat the oven to 200°C/400°F/ Gas 6. Scrub and dry the potatoes, and prick the skins with a fork or the tip of a sharp knife to prevent them bursting during cooking.

2 Rub the skins with oil and sprinkle with a little salt (if using).

3 Put the potatoes in the preheated oven, either on a baking sheet or straight onto the oven shelf. Cook for about 1 hour or until they are soft throughout – test by inserting a sharp knife into the centre.

4 Leave the cooked potatoes to stand for 5 minutes to cool slightly before splitting them open. Be careful of the escaping steam.

5 Serve with a dollop of butter on top, or sour cream and a sprinkling of parsley or chives.

Cook's tip If you are cooking a large number of potatoes in the oven, you will probably need to extend the cooking time by 10–15 minutes.

Energy 403kcal/1689kJ; Protein 5.4g; Carbohydrate 51.5g, of which sugars 2.9g; Fat 14.5g, of which saturates 6.1g; Cholesterol 0mg; Calcium 19mg; Fibre 3.7g; Sodium 59mg

Energy 182kcal/772kJ; Protein 3.8g; Carbohydrate 36.2g, of which sugars 2.9g; Fat 3.4g, of which saturates 0.6g; Cholesterol 0mg; Calcium 14mg; Fibre 2.3g; Sodium 25mg

Spiced roasted pumpkin

Pumpkins are traditionally hollowed out to make lanterns at Halloween, and the flesh is used in a number of delicious recipes, including pies and pickles. Here chunks of pumpkin are roasted with spices and herbs before being topped with cheese. Serve with a salad of watercress and baby spinach leaves. Minus the cheese, this side dish makes a good accompaniment to roast meats, sausages or lamb chops.

Serves 3–4

5ml/1 tsp fennel seeds

30ml/2 tbsp olive oil

1 garlic clove, crushed

5ml/1 tsp ground ginger

5ml/1 tsp dried thyme

pinch of chilli powder (optional)

salt and ground black pepper

piece of pumpkin weighing about 1.5kg/3lb 6oz

75g/3oz/¾ cup cheese, such as Cheddar, grated

1 Preheat the oven to 200°C/400°F/ Gas 6. Lightly crush or bruise the fennel seeds using a pestle and mortar, a rolling pin or the back of a large spoon – this process helps to release their flavour and improves the taste of the finished dish.

2 Put the oil into a large mixing bowl and stir in the fennel, garlic, ginger, thyme and chilli, if using. Season with salt and pepper and mix well.

3 Cut the skin off the pumpkin, scrape out and discard the seeds. Cut the flesh into rough chunks of about 3.5cm/1in. Toss the chunks in the oil mixture until evenly coated, then spread them in a single layer on a large baking tray.

4 Put into the hot oven and cook for about 40 minutes or until tender and golden brown on the edges. It helps to turn them over once during cooking.

5 Sprinkle the cheese over the top and return to the oven for 5 more minutes.

6 Serve straight from the baking tray, making sure all the golden bits of cheese are scraped up with the pumpkin.

Energy 171kcal/712kJ; Protein 7.1g; Carbohydrate 8.3g, of which sugars 6.4g; Fat 12g, of which saturates 5g; Cholesterol 17mg; Calcium 238mg; Fibre 3.8g; Sodium 127mg

Onion cake

Serve this simple but delicious dish as a snack accompanied with a fresh green salad. It's also particularly good alongside sausages, lamb chops or roast chicken – in fact, any roast meat. The cooking time will depend on the potatoes and how thinly they are sliced: use a food processor or mandolin (if you have one) to make paper-thin slices. The mound of potatoes will cook down to make a thick buttery cake.

Serves 6

900g/2lb new potatoes, peeled and thinly sliced

2 medium onions, very finely chopped

salt and ground black pepper

about 115g/4oz/½ cup butter

1 Preheat the oven to 190°C/375°F/ Gas 5. Butter a 20cm/8in round cake tin (pan) and line the base with a circle of baking parchment.

2 Arrange some of the potato slices evenly in the bottom of the tin and then sprinkle some of the onions over them. Season with salt and pepper. Reserve 25g/1oz/2 tbsp of the butter and dot the mixture with tiny pieces of the remaining butter.

3 Repeat these layers, using up all the ingredients and finishing with a layer of potatoes. Melt the reserved butter and brush it over the top.

4 Cover the potatoes with foil, put in the hot oven and cook for 1–1½ hours, until tender and golden. Remove from the oven and leave to stand, still covered, for 10–15 minutes.

5 Carefully turn out the onion cake on to a warmed plate and serve.

Cook's tip
If using old potatoes, cook and serve in an earthenware or ovenproof glass dish. Then remove the cover for the final 10–15 minutes to lightly brown the top.

Energy 272kcal/1133kJ; Protein 3.5g; Carbohydrate 29.5g, of which sugars 5.8g; Fat 16.3g, of which saturates 10.1g; Cholesterol 41mg; Calcium 29mg; Fibre 2.4g; Sodium 135mg

Pease pudding

This dish probably dates back to the 17th century, when puddings were boiled, wrapped in a cloth, in a pot alongside meat. Once a staple, it is still popular in the north-east of England.

Serves 6

450g/1lb dried split yellow peas

40g/1½ oz/3 tbsp butter, cut into pieces

1 egg, lightly beaten

salt and ground black pepper, to taste

1 Put the dried split yellow peas in a bowl and cover with cold water. Leave to soak for several hours or overnight.

2 Drain the peas thoroughly in a sieve (strainer) under cold running water. Place them into a pan.

3 Cover with fresh cold water, bring to the boil and simmer gently for about 45 minutes or until very soft.

4 Preheat the oven to 180°C/350°F/Gas 4. Drain the peas in a colander, then purée them to a smooth paste in a food processor or blender.

5 Add the butter, egg and seasoning, mix to combine thoroughly, then spoon into a buttered ovenproof dish.

6 Put the dish into the hot oven and cook for about 30 minutes until the pudding is set.

Cook's tips Pease pudding can also be steamed. Simply transfer the mixture to a pudding bowl at the end of step 5, cover with baking parchment and foil, and steam for about 45 minutes.
• A small handful of chopped fresh mint can be added to the purée in step 5.

Mushy peas

Dried marrowfat peas cooked and served in their own juice are believed to have originated in the north of England. Today, they are popular all over the country, especially with fish and chips. In the West Riding of Yorkshire mushy peas are served with pork pie.

Serves 4–6

250g/9oz dried peas

1 small onion

1 small carrot

2.5ml/½ tsp sugar

25g/1oz/2 tbsp butter

salt and ground black pepper, to taste

1 Put the peas in a bowl and pour over boiling water to cover them well. Soak for about 12 hours or overnight.

2 Drain and rinse the peas and put into a pan. Add the onion, carrot, sugar and 600ml/1pint/2½ cups cold water. Bring to the boil and simmer gently for about 20 minutes or until the peas are soft and the water absorbed.

3 Remove the onion and carrot from the pan. Mash the peas, seasoning to taste with salt and black pepper, and stir in the butter.

Cook's tip Cooking the peas in a muslin (cheesecloth) bag in step 2 stops them disintegrating.

Energy 300kcal/1270kJ; Protein 18.9g; Carbohydrate 42.3g, of which sugars 1.8g; Fat 7.4g, of which saturates 3.9g; Cholesterol 46mg; Calcium 44mg; Fibre 3.7g; Sodium 79mg

Energy 68kcal/288kJ; Protein 4.8g; Carbohydrate 11.5g, of which sugars 1.4g; Fat 0.6g, of which saturates 0.1g; Cholesterol 0mg; Calcium 12mg; Fibre 1.5g; Sodium 283mg

Braised leeks with carrots

Sweet carrots and leeks go well together and are good finished with a little chopped mint, chervil or parsley. This is an excellent accompaniment to roast beef, lamb or chicken.

Serves 4

70g/2½oz/5 tbsp butter

675g/1½lb carrots, thickly sliced

2 fresh bay leaves

pinch of sugar

675g/1½lb leeks, cut into 5cm/2in lengths

125ml/4fl oz/½ cup white wine

30ml/2 tbsp chopped fresh mint, chervil or parsley

salt and ground black pepper, to taste

1 Melt 25g/1oz/2 tbsp of the butter in a wide, heavy pan and cook the carrots, without allowing them to brown, for about 5 minutes. Add the bay leaves, seasoning, a pinch of sugar and 75ml/ 5 tbsp water.

2 Bring to the boil, cover and cook for 10 minutes, or until the carrots are just tender.

3 Uncover the pan and boil until the juices have evaporated, leaving the carrots moist and glazed. Remove from the pan and set aside.

4 Melt 25g/1oz/2 tbsp of the remaining butter in the pan. Add the leeks and cook over a low heat for 4–5 minutes, without allowing them to brown.

5 Add seasoning, a good pinch of sugar, the wine and half the chopped herbs. Heat until simmering, then cover and cook gently for 5–8 minutes, until the leeks are tender but not collapsed. Uncover and turn the leeks in the buttery juices, then increase the heat and boil the liquid rapidly until reduced to a few tablespoonfuls.

6 Add the carrots to the leeks in the pan and reheat gently, stirring occasionally, then add the remaining butter. Taste, then adjust the seasoning as required.

7 Transfer to a warmed serving dish and serve sprinkled with the remaining chopped herbs.

Energy 163kcal/677kJ; Protein 3.8g; Carbohydrate 18.5g, of which sugars 16.4g; Fat 6.5g, of which saturates 3.6g; Cholesterol 13mg; Calcium 87mg; Fibre 7.8g; Sodium 85mg

Spiced asparagus kale

Kale is a very important part of Scottish tradition. 'Kailyards' was the word used to describe the kitchen garden, and even the midday meal was often referred to as 'kail'. Use the more widely available curly kale if you find it hard to get the asparagus variety.

Serves 4

175g/6oz asparagus kale

10ml/2 tsp butter

25g/1oz piece fresh root ginger, grated

15ml/1 tbsp soy sauce

salt and ground black pepper

1 Prepare the kale by removing the centre stalk and ripping the leaves into smallish pieces.

2 Heat a pan over a high heat and add the butter. As it melts quickly add the kale and toss rapidly to allow the heat to cook it.

3 Grate the ginger into the pan and stir in thoroughly. Then add the soy sauce and mix well. When the kale has wilted, it is ready to serve.

Energy 35kcal/145kJ; Protein 1.6g; Carbohydrate 0.9g, of which sugars 0.9g; Fat 2.8g, of which saturates 1.4g; Cholesterol 5mg; Calcium 58mg; Fibre 1.4g; Sodium 301mg

Braised red cabbage

Red cabbage is a hardy vegetable that can be grown in a garden plot even in the difficult conditions of the highlands and islands of Scotland. Lightly spiced with a sharp, sweet flavour, braised red cabbage goes well with roast pork, duck and game dishes.

Serves 4–6

1kg/2¼lb red cabbage

2 cooking apples

2 onions, chopped

5ml/1 tsp freshly grated nutmeg

1.5ml/¼ tsp ground cloves

1.5ml/¼ tsp ground cinnamon

15ml/1 tbsp soft dark brown sugar

45ml/3 tbsp red wine vinegar

25g/1oz/2 tbsp butter, diced

salt and ground black pepper

chopped flat leaf parsley, to garnish

2 Layer the shredded cabbage in a large ovenproof dish with the onions, apples, spices, sugar, and salt and ground black pepper. Pour over the vinegar and add the diced butter.

3 Cover the dish with a lid and cook in the preheated oven for about 1½ hours, stirring a couple of times, until the cabbage is very tender. Serve immediately, garnished with the parsley.

1 Preheat the oven to 160°C/325°F/ Gas 3. Cut away and discard the large white ribs from the outer cabbage leaves using a large, sharp knife, then finely shred the cabbage. Peel, core and coarsely grate the apples.

Cook's Tip
This dish can be cooked in advance. Bake the cabbage for 1½ hours, then leave to cool. Store in a cool place covered with clear film (plastic wrap). To complete the cooking, bake it in the oven at 160°C/325°F/Gas 3 for about 30 minutes, stirring occasionally.

Energy 160kcal/668kJ; Protein 4.3g; Carbohydrate 23.8g, of which sugars 22.4g; Fat 5.8g, of which saturates 3.3g; Cholesterol 13mg; Calcium 140mg; Fibre 6.6g; Sodium 58mg

Desserts and baking

British people love sweet foods, and desserts play an important role in family meals. Many of these are based on seasonal ingredients, including berries and orchard and hedgerow fruits, or dairy products such as milk, buttermilk and cream. Regional and national breads, cakes and biscuits are also very popular, and home-baking is still part of everyday life for many people.

Cranachan

This lovely dish is based on a traditional Scottish recipe originally made to celebrate the Harvest Festival. It can be enjoyed as a teatime treat or a dessert, but it is also excellent served for breakfast or brunch. Try blueberries or blackberries in place of the raspberries.

Serves 4

75g/3oz crunchy oat cereal

600ml/1 pint/2½ cups Greek (US strained plain) yogurt

250g/9oz/1⅓ cups raspberries

heather or any other good-quality honey, to serve

1 Preheat the grill (broiler) to high. Spread the oat cereal on a baking sheet and place under the hot grill for 3–4 minutes, stirring regularly. Set aside on a plate to cool.

2 When the toasted cereal has cooled completely, fold it into the Greek yogurt, then gently fold in 200g/7oz/ generous 1 cup of the raspberries, being careful not to crush them. Reserve the remaining raspberries.

3 Spoon the yogurt mixture into four serving glasses or dishes, top with the remaining raspberries and serve immediately. Pass around a dish of heather honey to drizzle over the top for extra sweetness and flavour.

Variations
• You can use almost any berries for this recipe. Strawberries and blackberries work very well. If you use strawberries, remove the stalks and cut them into quarters beforehand.
• If you feel especially decadent, you can use clotted cream instead of yogurt, or try a mixture of half-and-half.

Energy 276kcal/1152kJ; Protein 12.4g; Carbohydrate 17.2g, of which sugars 11.1g; Fat 19.7g, of which saturates 8.7g; Cholesterol 0mg; Calcium 255mg; Fibre 2.5g; Sodium 122mg

Syllabub

This dish can be traced back to the 17th century, when it is said to have been made by pouring fresh milk, straight from the cow, on to spiced cider or ale, creating a frothy foam. Later, cream and wine were used to make an impressive and luxurious dessert.

Serves 6

1 orange

65g/2½oz/⅓ cup caster (superfine) sugar

60ml/4 tbsp medium dry sherry

300ml/½ pint/1¼ cups double (heavy) cream

strips of crystallized orange, to decorate

sponge fingers or crisp biscuits (cookies) to serve

1 Finely grate 2.5ml/½ tsp rind from the orange, then squeeze out its juice.

2 Put the orange rind and juice, sugar and sherry into a large bowl and stir until the sugar is completely dissolved. Stir in the cream. Whip the mixture until thick, and soft peaks form.

3 Spoon the syllabub into wine glasses with a teaspoon.

4 Chill the glasses of syllabub until ready to serve, then decorate with strips of crystallized orange. Serve with sponge fingers or crisp biscuits.

Cook's Tips Syllabub is also lovely spooned over a bowl of fresh soft fruit such as strawberries, apricots, raspberries or blackberries.
• You could try adding a pinch of ground cinnamon to the mixture in step 2.

Energy 310kcal/1282kJ; Protein 1.1g; Carbohydrate 14.5g, of which sugars 14.5g; Fat 26.9g, of which saturates 16.7g; Cholesterol 69mg; Calcium 41mg; Fibre 0.3g; Sodium 15mg

Rhubarb fool

This quick and simple dessert makes the most of field-grown rhubarb when it is in season. At other times of the year you could use different fruits. Serve with shortbread and pass around a dish of heather honey for those with a sweet tooth to drizzle over.

1 Cut the rhubarb into pieces and wash thoroughly. Stew over a low heat with just the water clinging to it and the sugar. This takes about 10 minutes. Set aside to cool.

2 Pass the rhubarb through a fine sieve (strainer) so you have a thick purée.

Serves 4

450g/1lb rhubarb, trimmed

75g/3oz/scant ½ cup soft light brown sugar

whipped double (heavy) cream and ready-made thick custard (see Step 3)

Variations
• You can use another fruit if you like for this dessert – try blackberries, gooseberries or apples. Other stewed fruits also work well, such as prunes or peaches. For something a little more exotic, you can use mangoes.
• For a low-fat option, substitute natural (plain) yogurt for the cream.

3 Use equal parts of the purée, the double cream and thick custard. Combine the purée and custard first then fold in the cream. Chill in the refrigerator before serving. Serve with heather honey.

Energy 439kcal/1828kJ; Protein 4.6g; Carbohydrate 34.1g, of which sugars 31.8g; Fat 31.7g, of which saturates 18.9g; Cholesterol 80mg; Calcium 233mg; Fibre 1.6g; Sodium 74mg

Summer pudding

This simple pudding is wonderfully easy to make, traditionally made with leftover breads and a few handfuls of garden and hedgerow berries. You could use thawed, frozen summer berries if you want to make it when fresh ones are not available.

Serves 4–6

8 x 1cm/½in thick slices of day-old white bread, crusts removed

800g/1¾lb/6–7 cups mixed berries, such as strawberries, raspberries, blackcurrants, redcurrants and blueberries

50g/2oz/¼ cup golden caster (superfine) sugar

lightly whipped double (heavy) cream or crème fraîche, to serve

1 Trim a slice of bread to fit in the base of a 1.2 litre/2 pint/5 cup bowl, then trim another 5–6 slices to line the sides of the bowl, making sure the bread comes up above the rim.

2 Place all the fruit in a pan with the sugar. Do not add any water. Cook for 4–5 minutes until the juices begin to run.

3 Allow the mixture to cool then spoon the berries, and enough of their juices to moisten, into the bread-lined bowl. Reserve any remaining juice.

4 Fold over the excess bread from the side of the bowl. Cover the fruit with the remaining bread, trimming the bread to fit.

5 Place a plate that fits inside the bowl directly on top of the pudding. Weight it down with a 900g/2lb weight, if you have one, or use a couple of full cans.

6 Chill in the refrigerator for at least 8 hours or overnight. Run a knife between the pudding and the bowl and turn out. Spoon any reserved juices over the top.

Energy 230kcal/977kJ; Protein 6.2g; Carbohydrate 51.7g, of which sugars 26.5g; Fat 1.2g, of which saturates 0g; Cholesterol 0mg; Calcium 98mg; Fibre 3g; Sodium 294mg

Apple pie

One of the nation's most popular desserts, apple pie features on many informal menus and, when well made, there is nothing to beat it. Bake in a traditional metal pie plate so that the pastry base will be perfectly cooked. Serve with whipped cream or vanilla ice cream.

Serves 6

225g/8oz/2 cups plain
(all-purpose) flour

130g/4½oz/generous ½ cup butter,
or mixed butter and white
vegetable fat (shortening)

25g/1oz/2 tbsp caster
(superfine) sugar

45ml/3 tbsp very cold milk or water

For the filling

675g/1½lb cooking apples

75g/3oz/½ cup sultanas
(golden raisins) (optional)

a little grated lemon rind (optional)

75g/3oz/6 tbsp caster
(superfine) sugar

a knob (pat) of butter or 15ml/
1 tbsp of water

a little milk, to glaze

icing (confectioners') sugar
and whipped cream, to serve

1 Sift the flour into a large mixing bowl and add the butter, or mixed butter and white vegetable fat, cut into small pieces. Rub the butter into the flour using the fingertips, lifting the mixture as much as possible to aerate it.

2 Mix the caster sugar with the chilled milk or water, add to the bowl and mix with a knife or fork until the mixture clings together. Turn on to a floured worktop and knead lightly once or twice until smooth.

3 Wrap in baking parchment or foil and leave in the refrigerator to relax for 20 minutes before using. Meanwhile, preheat the oven to 200°C/400°F/Gas 6.

4 Roll out one-third of the pastry and use to line a 23cm/9in pie plate. Use any trimmings to make a second layer of pastry around the top edge of the pie plate.

5 To make the filling, peel, core and slice the apples and arrange half of them on the pastry base, then sprinkle over the sultanas and lemon rind, if using. Top with the caster sugar, the remaining apples and butter or water.

6 Roll out the remainder of the pastry to make a circle about 2.5cm/1in larger than the pie plate. Dampen the pastry edging on the rim and lay the top over the apples, draping it gently over any lumps to avoid straining the pastry. Press the rim well to seal. Knock up the edge with a knife, and pinch it neatly with the fingers to make a fluted edge.

7 Brush the pastry lightly with milk and bake the pie in the preheated oven for about 30 minutes, or until the pastry is nicely browned and crisp, and the fruit is cooked.

8 Serve hot, warm or cold, but not straight from the refrigerator. Dust it with icing sugar, if you like.

Variation The same filling may be used to make a deep pie in a 25cm/10in deep oval pie dish, although only about three-quarters of the quantity of pastry will be needed for the topping.

Energy 393kcal/1650kJ; Protein 4.1g; Carbohydrate 56.3g, of which sugars 27.7g; Fat 18.4g, of which saturates 11.4g; Cholesterol 46mg; Calcium 68mg; Fibre 2.5g; Sodium 136mg

Raspberry and almond tart

Raspberries grow best in a cool, damp climate, making them a natural choice for many British gardeners. Juicy ripe raspberries and almonds go very well together, and the contrast of the rich custard with crisp pastry is fabulous. This is a rich tart, originally from Scotland, which is ideal for serving at the end of a special lunch or at a dinner party.

Serves 4

200g/7oz sweet pastry
(see Apple Pie, page 84)

2 large (US extra large) eggs

75ml/2½fl oz/⅓ cup double
(heavy) cream

50g/2oz/¼ cup caster
(superfine) sugar

50g/2oz/½ cup ground almonds

20g/¾oz/4 tsp butter

350g/12oz/2 cups raspberries

1 Line a 20cm/8in flan tin (tart pan) with the pastry. Prick the base all over and leave to rest for at least 30 minutes. Preheat the oven to 200°C/400°F/Gas 6.

2 Put the eggs, cream, sugar and ground almonds in a bowl and whisk together briskly. Melt the butter and pour into the mixture, stirring to combine thoroughly.

3 Sprinkle the raspberries evenly over the pastry case. The ones at the top will appear through the surface, so keep them evenly spaced. You can also create a pattern with them.

4 Pour the egg and almond mixture over the top. Once again ensure that it is spread evenly throughout the tart. Bake in the preheated oven for 25 minutes. Serve warm or cold.

Variation
Peaches make a very attractive and tasty tart. Use 6 large, ripe peaches and remove the skin and stone (pit). Cut into slices and use in the same way as the raspberries above.

Energy 548kcal/2284kJ; Protein 10.9g; Carbohydrate 41.7g, of which sugars 18.4g; Fat 38.8g, of which saturates 14.8g; Cholesterol 158mg; Calcium 128mg; Fibre 4.1g; Sodium 282mg

Bakewell tart

This is a modern version of the Bakewell pudding, which is made with puff pastry and has a custard-like almond filling. It is said to be the result of a 19th-century kitchen accident and is still baked in the original shop in Bakewell, Derbyshire. This very popular, tart-like version is simpler to make and is a favourite dessert and teatime treat all over Britain.

Serves 4

For the pastry

115g/4oz/1 cup plain (all-purpose) flour

pinch of salt

50g/2oz/4 tbsp butter, diced

For the filling

30ml/2 tbsp raspberry or apricot jam

2 whole eggs and 2 extra yolks

115g/4oz/generous ½ cup caster (superfine) sugar

115g/4oz/½ cup butter, melted

55g/2oz/⅔ cup ground almonds

few drops of almond extract

icing (confectioners') sugar, to dust

1 Sift the flour and salt and rub in the butter until the mixture resembles fine crumbs. Stir in about 20ml/2 tbsp cold water and gather into a smooth ball of dough. Wrap and chill for 30 minutes. Preheat the oven to 200°C/400°F/Gas 6.

2 Roll out the pastry and use to line an 18cm/7in loose-based flan tin (pan). Spread the jam over the pastry.

3 Whisk the eggs, egg yolks and sugar together in a large bowl until the mixture is thick and pale.

4 Gently stir in the melted butter, ground almonds and almond extract.

5 Pour the mixture over the jam in the pastry case (pie shell). Put the tart into the hot oven and cook for 30 minutes until just set and browned. Sift a little icing sugar over the top before serving warm or at room temperature.

Energy 700kcal/2919kJ; Protein 10.8g; Carbohydrate 57.1g, of which sugars 36.7g; Fat 49.9g, of which saturates 17.1g; Cholesterol 257mg; Calcium 110mg; Fibre 0.9g; Sodium 394mg

Plum crumble

The crumble is a perennially popular dessert, and is made with whichever seasonal fruits are available. Plums, used here, can be divided into three categories – dessert, dual and cooking. Choose whichever dual or cooking plum is grown locally. The addition of oats in the topping gives the crumble a nutty flavour and crunchy texture.

Serves 4

450g/1lb stoned (pitted) plums

50g/2oz/¼ cup soft light brown sugar

15ml/1 tbsp water

juice of 1 lemon

For the crumble topping

50g/2oz/½ cup plain (all-purpose) flour

25g/1oz/generous ¼ cup coarse rolled oats

50g/2oz/¼ cup soft light brown sugar

50g/2oz/¼ cup butter, softened

1 Preheat the oven to 200°C/400°F/ Gas 6. Put the plums in a large pan over a medium heat. Stir in the sugar, water and lemon juice. Bring to the boil, stirring continuously until the sugar dissolves. Cook the plums until they are just beginning to soften. Place the fruit with the juices in a deep pie dish.

2 Place the crumble ingredients in a bowl and mix with your fingers until the mixture resembles breadcrumbs.

3 Sprinkle the topping evenly over the fruit so that it is a good thickness. Bake in the preheated oven for 20 minutes, or until the top is crunchy and brown.

Energy 304kcal/1284kJ; Protein 2.9g; Carbohydrate 51.5g, of which sugars 37.4g; Fat 11.1g, of which saturates 6.5g; Cholesterol 27mg; Calcium 53mg; Fibre 2.8g; Sodium 82mg

Snowdon pudding

Reminiscent of a snow-capped mountain, this light pudding was allegedly created for a hotel situated at the base of Wales's highest peak. Use the softest, juiciest raisins you can find – they are more likely to stick to the bowl than small dry ones. This dessert is often served with a wine sauce – to make it, simply replace the milk with white wine.

Serves 6

15–25g/½–1oz/1–2 tbsp butter, softened

100g/3¾oz/⅔ cup raisins

175g/6oz/3 cups fresh white breadcrumbs

75g/3oz/½ cup shredded suet (US chilled, grated shortening)

75g/3oz/6 tbsp soft brown sugar

25g/1oz/¼ cup cornflour (cornstarch)

finely grated rind of 1 lemon

2 eggs

60ml/4 tbsp orange marmalade

30ml/2 tbsp fresh lemon juice

For the sauce

1 lemon

25g/1oz/¼ cup cornflour (cornstarch)

300ml/½ pint/1¼ cups milk

50g/2oz/¼ cup caster (superfine) sugar

25g/1oz/2 tbsp butter

2 Mix together the breadcrumbs, suet, brown sugar, cornflour, lemon rind and the remaining raisins. Beat the eggs with the marmalade and lemon juice and stir into the dry ingredients.

3 Spoon the mixture into the bowl, without disturbing the raisins.

4 Cover with baking parchment (pleated) and then a large sheet of foil (also pleated). Tuck the edges under and press tightly to the sides. Steam over a pan of boiling water for 1¾ hours.

5 To make the sauce, pare two or three large strips of lemon rind and put into a pan with 150ml/¼ pint/⅔ cup water. Bring to the boil and simmer for 10 minutes. Discard the rind. Blend the cornflour with the milk and stir into the pan. Squeeze the juice from half the lemon. Add it to the pan with the sugar and butter. Heat until the sauce thickens and boils.

6 Turn the pudding out on to a warmed plate, spooning a little sauce over the top.

1 Smear the butter on the inside of a 1.2-litre/2-pint pudding bowl and press half the raisins on the buttered surface.

Energy 456kcal/1922kJ; Protein 7.7g; Carbohydrate 74.4g, of which sugars 43.4g; Fat 16.8g, of which saturates 8.6g; Cholesterol 82mg; Calcium 131mg; Fibre 1.1g; Sodium 304mg

Scones with jam and cream

Scones, often known as biscuits in the US, are thought to originate from Scotland, although they are popular throughout the British Isles. They are normally served as part of afternoon tea with jams, jellies and a dollop of thick clotted cream.

Makes about 12

450g/1lb/4 cups self-raising (self-rising) flour, or 450g/1lb/4 cups plain (all-purpose) flour and 10ml/2 tsp baking powder

5ml/1 tsp salt

50g/2oz/¼ cup butter, chilled and diced

15ml/1 tbsp lemon juice

about 400ml/14fl oz/1⅔ cups milk, plus extra to glaze

fruit jam and clotted cream or whipped double (heavy) cream, to serve

1 Preheat the oven to 230°C/450°F/ Gas 8. Sift the flour, baking powder, if using, and salt into a clean, dry mixing bowl. Add the diced butter and rub it into the flour with your fingertips until the mixture resembles fine, evenly textured breadcrumbs.

2 Whisk the lemon juice into the milk and leave for about 1 minute to thicken slightly, then pour into the flour mixture and mix quickly to form a soft but pliable dough. The wetter the mixture, the lighter the resulting scones will be, but if it is too wet they will spread during baking and lose their shape.

3 Knead the dough lightly to form a ball, then roll it out on a floured surface to a thickness of at least 2.5cm/1in. Using a 5cm/2in pastry (cookie) cutter, and dipping it into flour each time, stamp out 12 scones. Place them on a floured baking sheet. Re-roll any trimmings and cut out more scones if you can.

4 Brush the tops of the scones lightly with a little milk then bake in the preheated oven for about 20 minutes, or until risen and golden brown. Remove the baking sheet from the oven and wrap the scones in a clean dish towel to keep them warm and soft until ready to serve. Eat with your favourite fruit jam and a generous dollop of cream.

Variation
To make cheese scones, add 115g/4oz/1 cup of grated cheese (preferably Cheddar or another strong hard cheese) to the dough and knead it in thoroughly before rolling out.

Energy 170kcal/720kJ; Protein 4.5g; Carbohydrate 29.9g, of which sugars 2.1g; Fat 4.4g, of which saturates 2.6g; Cholesterol 11mg; Calcium 172mg; Fibre 1.2g; Sodium 338mg

Scottish morning rolls

These rolls are best served warm, as soon as they are baked. In Scotland they are a firm favourite for breakfast with a fried egg and bacon. They also go very well with a pat of fresh butter and an assortment of homemade jams and jellies.

Makes 10

450g/1lb/4 cups unbleached strong white bread flour, plus extra for dusting

10ml/2 tsp salt

20g/¾oz fresh yeast

150ml/¼ pint/⅔ cup lukewarm milk, plus extra for glazing

150ml/¼ pint/⅔ cup lukewarm water

1 Grease two baking sheets. Sift the flour and salt together into a large bowl and make a well in the centre.

2 Mix the yeast with the milk, then mix in the water. Stir to dissolve.

3 Add the yeast mixture to the centre of the flour and mix together to form a soft dough.

4 Knead the dough lightly then cover loosely with lightly oiled clear film (plastic wrap) and leave to rise in a warm place for 1 hour, or until doubled in size.

5 Turn the dough out on to a floured surface and knock back (punch down).

6 Divide the dough into 10 equal pieces. Knead each roll lightly.

7 Using a rolling pin, shape each piece to a flat 10 x 7.5cm/4 x 3in oval or a flat 9cm/3½in round.

8 Transfer the rolls to the prepared baking sheets and cover with oiled clear film. Leave to rise in a warm place for about 30 minutes. Meanwhile, preheat the oven to 200°C/400°F/Gas 6.

9 Remove the clear film – the rolls should have risen slightly.

10 Press each roll in the centre with your three middle fingers to equalize the air bubbles and to help prevent blistering.

11 Brush with milk and dust with flour. Bake for 15–20 minutes, or until the tops are lightly browned.

12 As soon as you have removed them from the oven, dust with flour and cool slightly on a wire rack. Serve warm.

Energy 160kcal/682kJ; Protein 4.7g; Carbohydrate 35.7g, of which sugars 1.4g; Fat 0.8g, of which saturates 0.3g; Cholesterol 1mg; Calcium 81mg; Fibre 1.4g; Sodium 401mg

Traditional bara brith

Bara brith means 'speckled bread' in Welsh and that's just what this is – spicy yeasted bread speckled with dried fruit that has been plumped up in tea. Early types were likely to have been made from dough left over from bread making, with every family having its own favourite version. Serve it sliced thickly and spread with salty butter.

Makes 1 large loaf

225g/8oz/1⅓ cups mixed dried fruit and chopped mixed (candied) peel

350ml/12fl oz/1½ cups hot strong tea, strained

450g/1lb/4 cups strong white bread flour

50g/2oz/4 tbsp soft brown sugar

5ml/1 tsp salt

2.5ml/½ tsp mixed (apple pie) spice

30ml/2¼ tsp easy-blend (rapid-mix) yeast

50g/2oz/¼ cup butter, melted

milk, to mix

1 Put the fruit into a heatproof bowl and pour the hot tea over it. Cover and leave to stand at room temperature for several hours or overnight.

2 Sift the flour, sugar, salt and mixed spice into a large warmed mixing bowl. Stir in the yeast.

3 Add the fruit and its liquid and the melted butter. Stir well until the mixture can be gathered together to make a ball of soft smooth dough, adding a little milk if necessary.

4 Mix and stretch the dough on a lightly floured surface until it becomes smooth, firm and elastic. Return to the cleaned bowl. Cover with oiled clear film (plastic wrap) and leave in a warm place for about 1½ hours, or until the dough has more or less doubled its size.

5 Grease a 900g/2lb loaf tin (pan) and line it with baking parchment.

6 Turn the risen dough on to a lightly floured surface, gently press the air out, and then shape it into a loaf. Put it, seam-side down, into the prepared tin. Cover with oiled clear film and leave it in a warm place for about 1–1½ hours until the loaf has again just about doubled in size.

7 Preheat the oven to 200°C/400°F/ Gas 6. Put into the hot oven and cook for about 40 minutes until well risen, golden brown and cooked through. To test, turn the loaf out of its tin and tap the underneath – it should sound hollow.

8 Turn out and cool on a wire rack.

Energy 2730kcal/11567kJ; Protein 49.7g; Carbohydrate 557.8g, of which sugars 214.9g; Fat 48.7g, of which saturates 27.5g; Cholesterol 110mg; Calcium 890mg; Fibre 18.9g; Sodium 2414mg

Yorkshire parkin

This moist ginger cake from Yorkshire is traditionally served cut into squares and dusted with icing sugar. In former days, when a quantity of parkin was being baked in one go, one batch was sometimes eaten hot with apple sauce as a dessert. The flavour improves with time, so it is best to eat it the day after it is made.

Makes 16–20 squares

300ml/½ pint/1¼ cups milk

225g/8oz/1 cup golden (light corn) syrup

225g/8oz/¾ cup black treacle (molasses)

115g/4oz/½ cup butter

50g/2oz/scant ¼ cup soft dark brown sugar

450g/1lb/4 cups plain (all-purpose) flour

2.5ml/½ tsp bicarbonate of soda (baking soda)

7.5ml/1½ tsp ground ginger

350g/12oz/4 cups medium oatmeal

1 egg, beaten

icing (confectioners') sugar, to dust

1 Preheat the oven to 180°C/350°F/ Gas 4. Gently heat together the milk, syrup, treacle, butter and sugar, stirring until smooth; do not boil. Grease a 20cm/ 8in square cake tin (pan) and line the base and sides with baking parchment.

Cook's tip The flavour and texture of the cake improves if it is wrapped in foil and stored in an airtight container for several days.

2 Sift the flour into a large bowl, then add the bicarbonate of soda, ginger and oatmeal. Make a well in the centre of the dry ingredients and add the beaten egg, then the warmed milk and treacle mixture.

3 Stir well to make a smooth batter. Pour into the tin and bake for about 45 minutes, until firm to the touch. Cool slightly in the tin, then turn out to cool completely. Cut into squares and dust with icing sugar.

Energy 273kcal/1152kJ; Protein 5.3g; Carbohydrate 50g, of which sugars 20.1g; Fat 7.1g, of which saturates 3.3g; Cholesterol 23mg; Calcium 127mg; Fibre 1.9g; Sodium 102mg

Shortbread

The quintessential, originally Scottish, snack, shortbread is a great speciality and favourite. Made with butter and almonds, it is wonderfully rich and crumbly, perfect for serving with a cup of tea or coffee. The addition of lemon rind helps cut the sweetness.

3 Place the mixture on the oiled tray and flatten it out with a palette knife or metal spatula until evenly spread. Bake in the preheated oven for 20 minutes, or until pale golden brown.

4 Remove from the oven and immediately mark the shortbread into fingers or squares while the mixture is soft. Allow to cool a little, then transfer to a wire rack and leave until cold. Store in an airtight container for up to two weeks.

Cook's Tip
To make by hand, sift the flour and almonds on to a pastry board or work surface. Cream together the butter and sugar in a mixing bowl and then turn the creamed mixture on to the pastry board with the flour and almonds. Work the mixture together using your fingertips. It should come together to make a smooth dough. Continue as above from Step 3.

Makes about 48 fingers

oil, for greasing

275g/10oz/2½ cups plain (all-purpose) flour

25g/1oz/¼ cup ground almonds

225g/8oz/1 cup butter, softened

75g/3oz/scant ½ cup caster (superfine) sugar

grated rind of ½ lemon

1 Preheat the oven to 180°C/350°F/ Gas 4. Lightly oil a large Swiss roll tin (jelly roll pan) or baking tray.

2 Put the remaining ingredients into a blender or food processor and pulse until the mixture just comes together into a ball.

Variation
You can replace the lemon rind with the grated rind of two oranges for a tangy orange flavour, if you prefer.

Energy 64kcal/266kJ; Protein 0.7g; Carbohydrate 6.1g, of which sugars 1.8g; Fat 4.2g, of which saturates 2.5g; Cholesterol 10mg; Calcium 11mg; Fibre 0.2g; Sodium 29mg

Jam tarts

'The Queen of Hearts, she made some tarts, all on a summer's day; the Knave of Hearts, he stole those tarts, and took them quite away!' goes the nursery rhyme. Jam tarts have long been a treat at birthday parties and are often a child's first attempt at baking.

Makes 12

175g/6oz/1½ cups plain (all purpose) flour

pinch of salt

30ml/2 tbsp caster (superfine) sugar

85g/3oz/6 tbsp butter, diced

1 egg, lightly beaten

jam

1 Sift the flour and salt and stir in the sugar. Rub in the butter until the mixture resembles fine crumbs. Stir in the egg and gather into a smooth dough ball.

2 Chill the pastry ball for 30 minutes. Meanwhile, preheat the oven to 220°C/425°F/Gas 7 and lightly grease a 12-hole bun tray.

3 Roll out the pastry on a lightly floured surface to about 3mm/⅛in thick and, using a 7.5/3in fluted biscuit (cookie) cutter, cut out 12 circles. Press the pastry circles into the prepared tray. Put a teaspoonful of jam into each.

4 Put into the hot oven and cook for 15–20 minutes until the pastry is cooked and light golden brown. Carefully lift the tarts on to a wire rack and leave to cool before serving.

Mince pies

These small pies have become synonymous with Christmas. To eat one per day for the 12 days of Christmas was thought to bring happiness for the coming year.

Makes 12

225g/8oz/2 cups plain (all-purpose) flour

pinch of salt

45ml/3 tbsp caster (superfine) sugar, plus extra for dusting

115g/4oz/½ cup butter, diced

1 egg, lightly beaten

about 350g/12oz mincemeat

1 Sift the flour and salt and stir in the sugar. Rub in the butter until the mixture resembles fine crumbs. Stir in the egg and gather into a smooth dough.

2 Chill the pastry for 30 minutes. Meanwhile, preheat the oven to 220°C/425°F/Gas 7 and lightly grease a 12-hole bun tray.

3 Roll out the pastry on a lightly floured surface to about 3mm/⅛in thick and, using a 7.5/3in cutter, cut out 12 circles. Press into the prepared tray. Gather up the offcuts and roll out again, cutting slightly smaller circles to make 12 lids. Spoon mincemeat into each case, dampen the edges and top with a pastry lid. Make a small slit in each pie.

4 Bake for 15–20 minutes until light golden brown. Transfer to a wire rack to cool and serve dusted with sugar.

Energy 114kcal/479kJ; Protein 1.1g; Carbohydrate 18.8g, of which sugars 12.5g; Fat 4.3g, of which saturates 2.6g; Cholesterol 18mg; Calcium 16mg; Fibre 0.3g; Sodium 39mg

Energy 236kcal/993kJ; Protein 2.5g; Carbohydrate 36.7g, of which sugars 22.4g; Fat 9.8g, of which saturates 5.2g; Cholesterol 37mg; Calcium 43mg; Fibre 1g; Sodium 70mg

Index